ORVIS®

Guide to Great
SPORTING LODGE
Cuisine

BY JIM LEPAGE & PAUL FERSEN

PHOTOGRAPHS BY BRUCE CURTIS & *f*-STOP FITZGERALD
Produced by BAND-F Ltd.

THOMAS NELSON
Since 1798

NASHVILLE   DALLAS   MEXICO CITY   RIO DE JANEIRO   BEIJING

Band-f Ltd. President: f-stop Fitzgerald
Development Director: Karen Jones
Production Director: Mie Kingsley
Book Design: David Perry and Jason Cring
Production: Teal Hutton and Robin Dana
Director of Photography: Bruce Curtis

Select photographs from this book are available via our websites,
www.band-f.com or www.f-stopfitzgerald.com

Published in Nashville, Tennessee, by Thomas Nelson. Thomas Nelson is a trademark of Thomas Nelson, Inc.

Thomas Nelson, Inc., titles may be purchased in bulk for educational, business, fundraising, or sales promotional use.
For information, please e-mail SpecialMarkets@ThomasNelson.com.

Library of Congress Cataloging-in-Publication Data

Lepage, Jim.
  Orvis guide to great sporting lodge cuisine / Jim Lepage and Paul
Fersen ; photographs by Bruce Richard Curtis and F-Stop Fitzgerald.
      p. cm.
  Includes index.
  ISBN: 978-1-4016-0328-1
  1. Cookery. 2. Cookery (Game) 3. Hunting lodges--United States--Guidebooks. 4. Hunting lodges--Canada--Guidebooks.
5. Fishing lodges--United States--Guidebooks. 6. Fishing lodges--Canada--Guidebooks. I. Fersen, Paul. II. Orvis Company.
III. Title.
TX714.L4545 2008
641.6'91--dc22

                          2007047783

                    Printed in Singapore
                08 09 10 11 12 13—5 4 3 2 1

CONTENTS

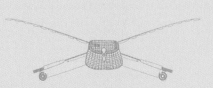

PREFACE

by Paul Fersen

There are those of us consumed by what we call the sporting traditions. For us, holding a beautifully figured walnut stock on a fine side-by-side engenders as much, if a different emotion, as holding the one we love. We cherish them both and without them our lives would be much the lesser. For us, a bamboo rod is a work of art but, when bent with the weight of a fish, a masterpiece. For us, the frozen poise of a great pointer is admirable, the courage of a magnificent retriever through frozen rivers heroic, the flight of the wild game bird and the leap of a wild rainbow heart-stopping.

They are traditions, for they have been with us for generations. Born of the necessity to provide sustenance in the primeval forest, the desire to hunt and fish has evolved from necessity to inclination, but for the true sportsman, the desire is in the experience, not the result. The passion is in finding ourselves in our quarry's environs and not in our own, for we have failed miserably there. For the true sportsman, the wilderness is life and the loss of it crushing. For the creatures we hunt, their sacrifice is further life for they feed and sustains us, but we have obligation in every death of our creation to honor them for their sacrifice and protect and preserve their habitats that they can thrive in perpetuity. This is the mission in the heart of a true sportsman.

It is the great sporting lodges that preserve these traditions. As the world grows smaller and the wilderness shrinks, the sporting lodges become more and more important in preserving these wilderness areas and the wild environs in which our beloved prey thrive. Whether finding oneself in a DeHaviland Beaver dropping into an Alaskan lake or on horseback high in the River of No Return Wilderness, there is solitude and a soulful peace that one cannot find in any other way. Watching a river full of bright spawning salmon and understanding the epic journey they have taken, the end of which you are witnessing, gives us an understanding of our true insignificance, but at the same time inspires us to be significant in trying to preserve these last great places.

The lodge experience is one of great friendship and shared passion, for those who frequent these lodges all share the belief that there is no better place one can be, and these shared passions are most frequently expressed over a magnificent meal at the end of the day. Here the adventures and wondrous experiences are shared with those who most appreciate them. Here the quarry is honored and thanked through its consumption and the great satisfaction it brings is.

This book is dedicated to the lodges that preserve these sporting traditions, these habitats, these last vestiges of the true wilderness experience, and share them with all who visit.

INTRODUCTION

by Jim Lepage

I t has been a dream of mine to see this collection of great lodge recipes in print. This book is the culmination of many rewarding years at sporting lodges and on sporting trips where everything—the food, the wine, a long day in a field, a sunrise and sunset, and the company—all come together to form a unique and unforgettable experience at the dining table. A wonderful meal with hunting and fishing companions can salvage a tough day in the field or be the crowning touch after a particularly memorable day hunting or fishing. The Orvis brand symbolizes distinctive country living, world class customer service, and more than 150 years of sporting tradition heritage. Only the finest lodges in the country can aspire to be part of the Orvis Endorsed Lodge Program, and although the best hunting and fishing is a prerequisite, that is only the beginning. Each lodge must have the best qualified guides in the region, offer the best customer experience, be a leader in conservation, offer the pinnacle of sporting lodging and cuisine, and deliver those attributes day in, day out without fail. Annual Orvis customer surveys of each lodge are the best information the lodges can receive to maintain their quality because the Orvis customer has the final word. As Chairman Leigh Perkins once said, "The customer is always right, even when you know damn well he's wrong."

Orvis Great Sporting Lodges and the Orvis Endorsed Lodge Program network is truly the best in the world, offering the best experience in hunting, fishing, and other field sports.

There are more than 80 Orvis-endorsed fly fishing and wingshooting lodges in North America, but these 41 are some of the more interesting. More than 140 recipes as unique as the lodges themselves are found in this cookbook. Each lodge supplied those recipes that have become favorites of the guests over the years. These recipes create a cookbook that is a unique culinary collection from the very best North American sporting lodges. You will find not only the finest in game recipes, but also side dishes, desserts, salads, appetizers, and other non-game entrees that will turn your dining experience into a sporting tradition.

Reading this book, you will also get to know each of these great sporting lodges, the history, and the world-class fishing or hunting they provide. To experience these lodges, Paul Fersen takes you on a journey to each lodge, creating the unique feeling that you are at the lodge, seeing what a guest would see, and feeling what is like to take part in the sporting experience the lodge has to offer. You will be able to envision what it is like to sit on the front porch of Libby's Camps (2007 Endorsed Fly Fishing Lodge of the Year) and watch the sunset deep in the north Maine woods before sitting down to enjoy the family-style food that Ellen and Jess Libby serve in their great log lodge. This is where the guests gather at the end of a day's grouse hunt or a day fishing the streams and ponds for the jeweled Maine brook trout.

You will also be able to experience a day on a quail wagon at Georgia's Wynfield Plantation. You can understand the excitement of a covey rise, the extraordinary work of the pointers and setters that have become part of this tradition, and learn the history so deeply rooted in the plantation experience. But at the end of a day, with dogs and friends in one of the greatest of Southern traditions, you can finally experience fine Georgia dining. Pictures from award-winning photographers Bruce Curtis and F-Stop Fitzgerald will show much of the cuisine presented in this book, as well as give life to the lodges.

The Orvis Great Sporting Lodges range from award-winning five-star dining at Blackberry Farm in Walland, Tennessee, Marquesas Hotel in Key West, Florida, or Firehole Ranch in Yellowstone, Montana, to the rustic lodges of Weatherby's on Grand Lake Stream, Maine, or North Fork Crossing on the Blackfoot River in Montana where you can experience "roughing it in style" in their unique tent camps. The lodges range from Maine to Montana, and from Alaska to Key West, Florida, and include Canadian lodges as well.

The easy-to-follow directions in the recipes will allow you to create and present the very best of the great sporting lodge cuisine in your own kitchen. Recreating these recipes for guests and recounting your own knowledge of the traditions and sporting heritage of the lodges where they are served makes for a rewarding and memorable dining experience.

The Orvis Guide to Great Sporting Lodge Cuisine fulfills a long-held vision to bring together the best these lodges have to offer for your own dining experience. Enjoy and bon appetite.

Jim Lepage

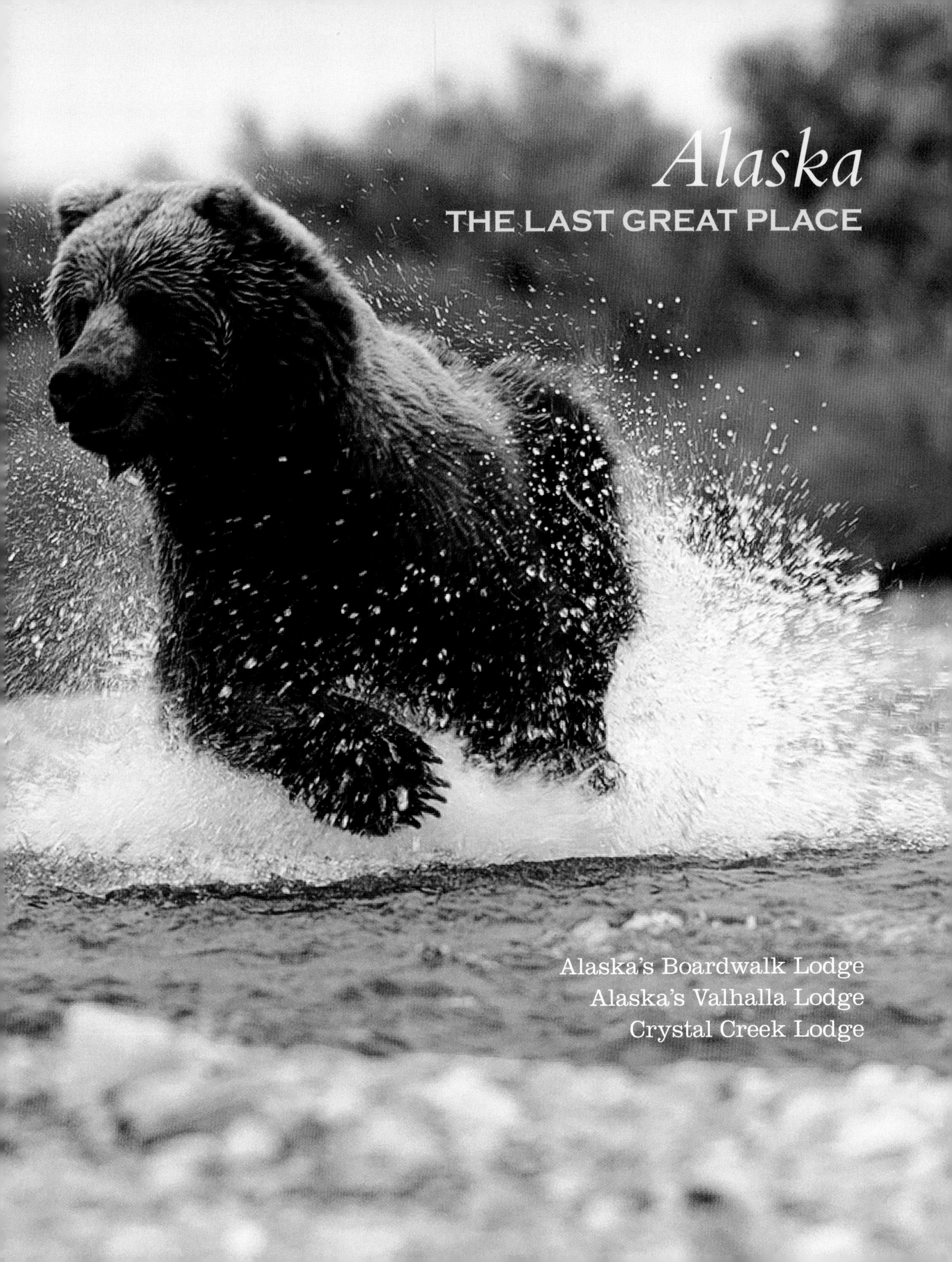

Alaska
THE LAST GREAT PLACE

Alaska's Boardwalk Lodge
Alaska's Valhalla Lodge
Crystal Creek Lodge

ALASKA'S BOARDWALK LODGE

Prince of Wales Island, Alaska

Until you actually set foot in Alaska it is impossible to understand the difference between the lower forty-eight states and this immense and varied frontier. The diversity of wildlife, the magnificence of the scenery, and the sheer majesty of a place so big are often overwhelming and add to Alaska's allure.

Alaska's Boardwalk Lodge lies on the shore of Prince of Wales Island, the third largest island in the United States after the big island of Hawaii and Alaska's own Kodiak. The island is one of the sliver of islands that run along the coast of Canada in Alaska's panhandle. What makes this area unique is that it is a temperate rainforest with extraordinary biodiversity and a climate that is hospitable for a great part of the year. That biodiversity combined with the five-star mentality of Boardwalk's staff makes for one of the finest sporting and naturalist destinations in the world.

Prince of Wales Island is a remarkable environment. Nearly all of the island is part of the Tongass National Forest, which encompasses nearly 2,600 square miles. What sets this island apart from other areas of Alaska is the accessibility to streams and small river systems, all teeming with steelhead trout and Pacific salmon. Rather than having to fly to destinations, a four-wheel-drive vehicle and a good guide can put an angler on water that may not have seen another angler that year and fish that have never seen a fly. The stories of steelhead attacking flies are reminiscent of some of the great stories of Maine's landlock salmon at the end of the nineteenth century. This is fishing that is unavailable anywhere in the lower forty-eight states.

Alaska's Boardwalk Lodge was built in 1990 on the eastern shore of Prince of Wales Island, nestled inside the cove of Thorne Bay. Each log was felled and towed across Thorne Bay where it was notched and peeled by hand, and over the course of seven years, the three-story lodge was completed. Today it is a showplace with rustically elegant rooms and unmatched cuisine. Arrival at the lodge is a ceremony, as the entire staff comes to the dock to greet guests, take their luggage, and then determine their guests' desires. Whatever is available, the staff will arrange.

Executive Chef Eric Shultz creates an Alaskan menu using local ingredients, from Dungeness crab to a variety of salmon, down to fresh blueberries. One of the notable touches when entering the dining room is the hand-lettered menu at each table. On each menu are the various courses for the meal, often with a personal note of congratulations to the day's most successful angler, or a welcome to the lodge's new guests. Alaska is magic, of that there is no question. Alaska's Boardwalk Lodge simply offers one of the best places to be astounded and amazed.

PAN-SEARED HALIBUT

4   6- to 8-ounce halibut fillets
     Salt and pepper to taste
1   tablespoon vegetable oil

Preheat the oven to 350°. Rub the halibut fillets with salt and pepper to taste.

In a large ovenproof sauté pan heat the vegetable oil on high heat. Add the halibut to the pan. When the bottom is a golden brown flip over and brown the other side.

Remove the sauté pan from the heat and place in the oven for 8 to 10 minutes. The halibut should flake with a fork when done.

Remove from the oven and serve with Lemon Risotto (recipe follows).

To serve, spoon the risotto on each plate and top with a halibut fillet.

Makes 4 servings.

LEMON RISOTTO

1   tablespoon butter
1   cup Arborio rice
2   tablespoons minced shallots
     Zest of one lemon
1   quart chicken broth

In a medium saucepan over medium heat melt the butter and add the shallots. Cook the shallots until just translucent. Add the rice and lemon zest. Add enough chicken broth to cover the rice and continue to stir. Add more chicken broth as it is absorbed by the rice and continue to stir for about 15 to 20 minutes. Continue to add chicken broth until all the broth has been absorbed or until the rice is done.

Makes 4 servings.

MARINATED CHICKEN BREASTS STUFFED WITH SPINACH AND GOAT CHEESE

Chicken

8	ounces fresh basil leaves (stems removed)
5	garlic cloves, peeled
1	cup olive oil
8	5- to 7-ounce boneless, skinless chicken breasts
8	ounces softened goat cheese
3	shallots, minced
8	ounces fresh spinach
1/2	cup heavy cream
	Vegetable oil

Sauce

1	tablespoon butter
1	quart heavy cream
8	ounces Brie cheese, rind removed and cut into pieces
2	pounds button mushrooms, stems removed and roughly chopped
	Salt and pepper to taste

Rice

1	cup basmati rice
1 1/2	cups water
1	teaspoon saffron
1	tablespoon butter
	Pinch salt
1/2	pound fresh snow peas, blanched

For the chicken, combine the fresh basil, garlic cloves, and olive oil in a blender and blend until smooth. Put the chicken breasts in a large bowl and pour the olive oil mixture over them. Toss the chicken, making sure that it is thoroughly coated. Cover with plastic and refrigerate for 2 hours.

Combine the goat cheese, minced shallots, and spinach in a large mixing bowl and beat on medium-low speed of a mixer. Add the heavy cream a little at a time until the mixture is loose enough to pipe through a bag.

Remove the chicken from the refrigerator. With a boning knife make a small incision in the chicken breast on the thick end, about 1 1/2 inches wide. Insert the knife about 3 inches and make a cavity for the stuffing, being sure not to puncture the meat. Place the spinach and goat cheese mixture in a piping bag. Insert the piping bag into the cavity and squeeze the filling into each breast. Secure the opening with a toothpick.

Preheat the oven to 350°. Over high heat cook the chicken in a small amount of vegetable oil in an ovenproof sauté pan (nonstick pans work best). Place the chicken in the pan and cook until brown. Flip the chicken over and brown the other side. Place in the oven for 10 to 12 minutes.

For the sauce, in a large saucepot melt the butter. Add the heavy cream and Brie and cook over low heat. Reduce the sauce by one-fourth. Pour the sauce into a blender container. Add the mushrooms. Purée the sauce, covering it with a towel to prevent burning. Add salt and pepper to taste.

For the rice, thoroughly rinse the rice. In a large saucepan add the rice, water, saffron, butter, and a pinch of salt. Bring to a boil and reduce to a simmer for 3 minutes. Cover and turn off the heat; let it stand for 15 minutes.

To serve, place a spoonful of the rice on one side of a plate. Put the snow peas on the opposite side of the plate. Offset the chicken on the plate so it is slightly on top of the rice. Ladle the cheese sauce over the chicken.

Makes 4 servings.

SWEET DUNGENESS CRAB AND SCALLOP-FILLED PUFF PASTRY

2   cups heavy cream
1   leek, cleaned, cut in half lengthwise, then sliced
12 4x4-inch puff pastry squares
1/2 pound Dungeness crabmeat (claw meat)
1/2 pound scallops (any size)
3   eggs, beaten

Cook the cream over medium–high heat and until reduced by half, stirring frequently, about 15 minutes. Set aside in the refrigerator to chill.

Blanch the leek in salted water. Immediately soak in ice water, drain, and set aside.

Cut the puff pastry squares in half diagonally. Combine the crab, scallops, chilled cream, and blanched leeks in a food processor and purée until smooth.

Preheat the oven to 400°. Place one half of a pastry square on a surface so that it looks like an upside-down triangle. Place about 1 teaspoon of the crab mixture in the middle of the triangle. Take the bottom point of the triangle and fold it over the mixture to the top edge of the triangle. With the remaining two points, fold them downward and close together so there is a seam down the middle. Turn the pastry over and fold the two points downward again so that the pastry forms a triangle.

Place the pastry on a sheet pan lined with parchment paper and brush with the beaten eggs. Place in the oven for 10 minutes. If the pastries aren't golden brown, leave them in for two more minutes or until brown.

Makes 6 to 8 appetizer servings.

ALASKA'S VALHALLA LODGE

Anchorage, Alaska

Ward Gay first arrived in Alaska in 1935 on a steamship in steerage class. By 1939 he had earned his pilot certificate and Alaska Guide License, and over the next forty years he built an extensive aviation business and guide service, flying throughout Alaska and hunting and fishing from the Alaska Peninsula, 400 miles south of Anchorage, to the Wrangell Mountains in the east, and above the Artic Circle in the north.

In 1955, Gay purchased a small parcel of lakefront land at the headwaters of the trout and salmon streams that feed Bristol Bay where millions of sockeye, silver, king, pink, and chum salmon return each year to spawn, feeding and nourishing an entire ecosystem. It is arguably the greatest fishing destination in the world for sheer magnitude of fishing area and variety of species to be caught. Gay's son Kirk was just eleven years old when his father bought the property. He spent his summers working there, and by the time he was fifteen he was flying and guiding clients on his own. In 1980 he took over the fish camp at Six Mile Lake and built his lodge, naming it after the legendary paradise for Viking warriors. All the logs and supplies for the new lodge were flown in by a World War II-era cargo plane, which landed on the ice during the winter, as this was the only way to access the property with large loads.

Today Valhalla is one of the finest and most renowned of Alaskan lodges. Floatplane fly-outs are available to remote destinations, where strategically placed jet boats take anglers even further into the bush to fish in magnificent untouched spots teeming with trout and salmon. Kirk's son Chris now carries on the tradition as chief guide for the lodge, pushing the family's expertise in this wilderness experience to the third generation.

June is a great month for rainbow trout, Arctic char, Arctic grayling, lake trout, and northern pike. By the middle of June chinook (king salmon) begin their migration into freshwater streams. This is a classic "dry fly" month for trout and grayling.

July offers rainbow trout, Arctic char, lake trout, grayling, and northern pike. The king salmon, sockeye salmon, and chum salmon are also entering the rivers by the millions. August provides rainbow trout, Arctic char, Dolly Varden, and grayling. Sockeye salmon fish well through the early part of the month. Coho (silver salmon), pink salmon, and chum salmon

are plentiful. By September, Arctic char and Dolly Varden have their beautiful fall spawning colors and big rainbow and silver trout are everywhere.

This is a true wilderness experience in the most majestic of settings. One cannot grasp the magnificence of Alaska from books. It is only from the seat of a floatplane, dancing between the peaks in search of remote waters that one truly understands the spectacular nature of this place, unlike anything the lower forty-eight states can offer. Valhalla sits amid the lakes and mountains, a secluded refuge from a busy world, with fishing that is unchanged from the time man first set foot on these rivers.

CAPTAIN KIRK'S SMOKED SALMON
SEAFOOD CHOWDER

Salsa

1	small fresh tomato, chopped
1	tablespoon chopped white onion
	Roasted jalapeño pepper to taste
	Cilantro to taste

Chowder

1	cup chopped white onion
1	cup chopped celery
1	cup salsa (see previous above)
1	tablespoon coarse black pepper
4	cups water
3	cups chopped peeled potatoes
	Pinch of salt
	Pinch of dried thyme and basil
1	cup deboned chunked smoked salmon
2	cups medium peeled cooked shrimp
2	cups small scallops
1	cup cooked chunked king crab leg meat
1	can evaporated milk
1	cup whole milk (add more as needed—chowder best if not too thick)
1	cup half-and-half
3	tablespoons butter
1/2	cup chopped fresh parsley
	Sprig of parsley for garnish

For the salsa, mix the tomato, onion, jalapeño, and cilantro in a small bowl. Cover and refrigerate.

For the chowder, in a 2-gallon pot with a lid slowly boil the onion, celery, salsa, and pepper over medium heat.

In a separate large pot, combine the water and potatoes. Add a pinch of salt. Bring to a boil and then rinse and drain twice. Add the potatoes to the vegetable stock and cook uncovered until soft. (Some of the potatoes can be mashed to yield a thicker stock to the chowder base.) Add the thyme, basil, salmon, shrimp, scallops, and crab. Slowly boil for 5 minutes.

Add evaporated milk and cook on low heat. Do not boil milk.

Add the whole milk, half-and-half, butter, and parsley. Cook on low heat being careful not to boil.

Flavor with sea salt as desired, and garnish with a sprig of fresh parsley.

Makes 16 appetizer or 8 entrée servings.

VALHALLA STUFFED SALMON FILLET

2	tablespoons chopped shallots
2	tablespoons chopped celery
1/4	cup butter or margarine
1	teaspoon orange oil
1	tablespoon honey
1	teaspoon dried basil
1	teaspoon ground black pepper
1/4	cup white wine
1/2	cup cooked small bay shrimp
1/2	cup cooked chopped crab leg meat
1	salmon fillet, deboned and skinned
	Clarified butter for brushing
1/4	cup toasted chopped pine nuts
	Orange and lemon slices for garnish

Preheat the oven to broil. Sauté the shallots and celery in the butter and orange oil. Stir in the honey and add the basil, pepper, white wine, shrimp, and crab. Mix well. Remove the pan from the heat and let sit to cool.

Slice the salmon fillet down the back (lay the fillet on a cutting board and slice down the back toward the belly) and stuff with the shrimp and crab mixture.

Place the fillet on a broiling pan and brush with clarified butter. Place on the top oven rack and broil for about 8 minutes. The salmon should be moist and flaky.

Place the fillet on a platter, sprinkle with the toasted pine nuts. After the presentation on the platter, cut fillet into 4 serving-size pieces. Garnish with orange and lemon slices. Serve with dill sauce and/or tartar sauce on the side.

Makes 4 servings.

VEAL MEDALLIONS WITH HUNTER SAUCE

Veal Medallions

1   veal loin
1/2 cup plus 2 tablespoons olive oil
1/2 cup white wine
1/2 cup butter
1   tablespoon firmly packed brown sugar
1   white onion, sliced
1/2 cup all-purpose flour

Hunter Sauce

2   tablespoons flour
2   tablespoons demi-glace powder
2   cups water
1/4 cup white wine
1/4 cup minced white onions
1/4 cup chopped mushrooms
1   tablespoon ground green peppercorns
1   tablespoon butter
1   tablespoon chopped fresh parsley
1   teaspoon chopped fresh thyme
1   teaspoon salt
     Parsley sprigs for garnish

For the veal, slice the veal loin into 1/4-inch-thick medallions. Pound lightly with a meat hammer. In a shallow dish, mix 1/2 cup of the olive oil and the wine and marinate the veal for 1 hour in the refrigerator.

Remove the medallions from the refrigerator and dry with paper towels. Discard the marinade.

Heat the butter and brown sugar in a saucepan. Add the onion and cook until lightly browned. Keep warm until ready to serve.

Dust the veal medallions with flour. In a skillet, heat the remaining 2 tablespoons olive oil and cook the medallions, flipping just once. Remove the medallions from the pan and keep them warm in the oven.

For the sauce, add the flour and demi-glace powder to the skillet used to cook the veal, mixing well with the remaining olive oil and veal drippings in the warm pan. Add the water, white wine, onions, mushrooms, green peppercorns, butter, parsley, thyme, and salt. Heat to a slow boil, stirring to reduce the liquid to make a medium-thick gravy.

Ladle the sauce onto the individual serving plates and place the medallions on top of the sauce. Garnish with a sprig of parsley.

Makes 8 appetizer servings.

CRÊPES À LA VALHALLA

French Crêpes

1/2　cup cake flour
1/2　cup milk
1　　teaspoon vanilla
1　　teaspoon honey
1　　tablespoon melted butter
1　　egg
　　　Vegetable oil

Filling

1/2　cup berries, divided
1/4　cup yogurt
1/2　teaspoon orange oil
3　　small scoops vanilla ice cream
　　　Whipped cream
1　　tablespoon crumbled walnuts
　　　Chocolate wafer crumbles

For the crêpes, in a mixing bowl combine the cake flour, milk, vanilla, honey, butter, and egg, and stir until the mixture is thin. Pour a small amount of the batter into a hot frying pan coated with vegetable oil to make a crêpe. Flip just once, much like making a pancake. Let the crêpes cool.

For the filling, combine 1/4 cup of the berries, the yogurt, and orange oil in a blender to make a puréed sauce.

Place one crêpe flat on a serving plate. Place the ice cream on the crêpe. Sprinkle some of the remaining berries and some of the puréed sauce over the ice cream. Roll the crêpe.

Add the remaining berries, the remaining puréed sauce, whipped cream, the crumbled walnuts, and chocolate wafer crumbles to the outside of the filled crêpe.

Makes 8 dessert servings.

CRYSTAL CREEK LODGE

King Salmon, Alaska

Any time a group of anglers swap lies and tell stories of their adventures on the rivers of the world, a number of ecosystems inevitably rise to the top of the conversation. The Florida Keys of course, Andros Island, the Russian salmon rivers, and Argentina are usually included. But of all the great destinations for anglers, one is extraordinary not only for the vastness of the region and the staggering numbers of fish, but for the incredible number of species.

That region is Bristol Bay, Alaska. Between the southwest Alaskan mainland to its north and the Alaska Peninsula to its south and east, Bristol Bay is 250 miles long and 180 miles wide at its mouth. The Cinder, Igushik, Kvichak, Meshik, Nushagak, Naknek, Togiak, and Ugashik rivers all flow into the bay, making it the epicenter of the pacific salmon culture and all the incredible species that these fish support in their spawning rituals.

Crystal Creek Lodge is a beautiful 7,500-square-foot structure offering visitors the opportunity to experience everything that the region has to offer. There is extraordinary fishing for eleven species of fish, including all five of the Pacific salmon species, rainbow trout, Dolly Varden, Arctic grayling, northern pike, and lake trout. Guests also enjoy hunting wild ptarmigan, ducks, and geese, wildlife viewing, kayaking, and even sky trekking, in which remote regions of the area are explored with a guide by air.

Dan and Lori Michels are the consummate Alaskan hosts because they do it all. They don't just own the lodge; they are guides and pilots, they know this region as well as anyone, and they love to share that experience with their guests. Their service is impeccable, and as Dan states, "Our guides are not there to fish, they are there to make sure the guests have everything they need."

This region is beyond spectacular. The salmon cycle and the culture and ecosystem it supports is one of the most fascinating in the world. It is described in an article in *Gray's Sporting Journal* by this author as follows:

In the back eddy next to me, a king drifted slowly toward the bank on her side. She had no fins to speak of, having worn them out clearing the silt from her nest. Her skin was pale and in the middle stages of decomposition. Her eye was cloudy and she was undoubtedly blind.

An almost imperceptible motion in what was left of her tail pushed her the last few inches to the gravel. I knelt beside her and watched her gills move slowly until finally they stopped. Seven years prior she left this river on an incomparable journey to the ocean, dodging predators, nets, and swimming thousands of miles in the Pacific, until something told her to come back. She again dodged and weaved her way through untold danger, wearing away her body on the gravel and ultimately finishing her life in the pool where she was born, completing the cycle. Her success was the eggs lying in the gravel. Her flesh would feed an ecosystem and sustain hundreds of other species. I was witnessing the death of a Homeric creature.

Crystal Creek Lodge is a place where they understand this and, more importantly, want to share it with their guests, for there is perhaps no greater lesson in how nature can be so magnificently self-sustaining.

ALASKAN AMBER AND DARK BEER BREAD

1/4 cup honey

1 1/2 cups Alaskan amber (or similar dark beer)

3 tablespoons active dry yeast

2 cups bread flour

1 cup whole wheat flour

1/4 cup quick cooking oats

4 tablespoons cocoa

2 tablespoons salt

1 1/2 teaspoons cumin

1 1/2 teaspoons coriander

Vegetable oil

Cornmeal

In a saucepan mix the honey and beer and warm to 105°. Add the yeast and let it sit for 5 minutes until foamy. Pour into a large mixing bowl.

In a separate bowl mix the flours, oats, cocoa, salt, cumin, and coriander. Add to the beer mixture using a mixer with a dough hook. Knead for approximately 10 minutes on medium speed; the dough should ball up and not stick to the side of the bowl. If the dough is sticking, add a little more flour. Remove the dough from the bowl and form into a ball.

Add a small amount of oil to a large bowl and roll the bread ball so that it is coated with oil. Cover the bowl with plastic wrap. In a warm area let the bread rise until doubled in size. Punch down and reform into a ball.

Preheat the oven to 420°. Sprinkle corn meal on a sheet pan and place the bread on the pan. Cover with plastic wrap and let it rise until approximately doubled in size. With a sharp knife make a tic-tac-toe pattern on top of the bread and sprinkle with a little flour. Bake for approximately 25 to 35 minutes. The bread is finished when you can tap the bottom and hear a hollow sound.

Makes 1 loaf.

CEDAR PLANK SALMON WITH BOURBON BIRCH SYRUP GLAZE

1 12x7-inch cedar or alder plank soaked in water

1 cup birch syrup (maple syrup may be substituted)

1/2 cup bourbon

2 tablespoons butter

Pinch salt

1 1 1/2-pound salmon fillet

Soak the cedar plank in water for 2 hours before using it.

Preheat the grill to high.

Cook the syrup and bourbon together in a small saucepan until glaze consistency, slightly thicker than the syrup by itself. Add the butter and a pinch of salt. Keep warm.

Place the salmon on the wet cedar plank and place on a very hot grill. Close the grill and cook the salmon to medium, about 8 to 10 minutes. Don't overcook or the salmon will be dry.

Ladle the glaze over the salmon and serve.

Makes 4 servings.

FLOURLESS CHOCOLATE ALMOND CAKE

Chocolate Cake

16 ounces milk chocolate morsels (such as Hershey's)

1 cup heavy cream

1 cup plus 2 tablespoons sugar, divided

1/2 cup (1 stick) unsalted butter

2 pinches salt

1 cup sliced toasted almonds

1 tablespoon vegetable oil

8 eggs at room temperature, separated

1/4 cup amaretto liquor

2 tablespoons sliced toasted almonds for garnish

Ganache Frosting

8 ounces semisweet chocolate morsels

3/4 cup heavy cream

2 tablespoons sugar

2 tablespoons unsalted butter

For the cake, in a saucepan over medium heat, melt the chocolate morsels, heavy cream, and 1/2 cup of the sugar until smooth, stirring constantly. Whisk in the butter. Add the salt, and set aside.

Mix 1 cup of the toasted almonds and the vegetable oil in a blender until smooth, adding more vegetable oil if needed. Stir the almonds into the melted chocolate.

In a mixing bowl whisk together the egg yolks and 2 tablespoons of the sugar until pale yellow and a ribbon forms when a small amount falls back into the bowl. Stir into the chocolate.

In a separate bowl beat the egg whites until medium peaks form. Add the remaining 1/2 cup sugar in thirds until hard peaks form. Fold the meringue into the chocolate by thirds.

Preheat the oven to 350°. Grease and flour a 15-inch springform pan. Pour the batter into the prepared pan. Bake for approximately 20 minutes. The cake will rise and crack at the top. Let it cool.

For the frosting, in a saucepan over medium-low heat melt the chocolate morsels, heavy cream, and sugar until smooth. Whisk in the butter. Cool.

To serve, pour the ganache on the cake until the center of the cake is covered, reserving some ganache for serving. Sprinkle 1 tablespoon of the toasted almonds around the edge of the cake.

Garnish each slice of cake with 1 teaspoon of the remaining ganache and sprinkle with the remaining toasted almonds. This cake is very rich and goes a long way.

Makes 16 servings.

Midwest
ENDLESS HEARTLAND

Dos Angeles Ranch
Legacy Ranch
Paul Nelson Farm

DOS ANGELES RANCH

Brackettville, Texas

os Angeles is one of those exceptional lodges that offer a total experience that other lodges just can't quite seem to attain. The reason is simply that owners Jack and Lynn Fields have assembled one of the most qualified and experienced staffs a lodge could hope to have.

Take, for instance, the executive chef, Carlos Gomez, who has been an executive chef for more than twenty years. His clientele includes the most powerful and the most demanding in the world. Among others, he has served the Speaker of the House of Representatives, the Senate Majority Leader, major committee chairmen of the House and Senate, ambassadors from around the world, the Prince of Lichtenstein, all of the former directors of the CIA, the former director of the Mossad, the CEOs of major American companies, and sports celebrities. Or consider the quail biologist whose sole duty is to maintain the quality of the quail hunting on Dos Angeles's 12,400 acres. Dale Rollins is the leading quail biologist in Texas and, given the list of his degrees, achievements, awards, and recognition for work in the field, easily one of the leading quail biologists in the world. His expertise keeps Dos Angeles as one of the great quail destinations in the world.

Pinto Creek flows three and a half miles through the property, and although Dos Angeles Ranch is only twelve miles from the Mexican border, this stream is pure Texas hill country water, flowing over limestone and creating excellent fishing opportunities in the deep holes and pools that rock falls have created

over the years. It was just below the ranch that *Lonesome Dove* was filmed and the ranch reflects that warm southwestern landscape dotted with cool river bottom glades. Constance Whiston is the fishing guide and habitat advisor for the ranch and is one of the most respected anglers in North America. She is an accomplished guide, writer, instructor, and lecturer.

This extraordinary team that Jack and Lynn Fields have assembled provide their guests with an unequaled total experience. From the minute guests enter the Mexican-inspired ranch, they are treated to the finest hospitality that south Texas can offer. The food is world-class, the accommodations are cool and inviting, the quail hunting is the best that a hunter could ask for, the fishing is excellent, the dogs are beautifully trained, and the countryside is wonderfully romantic in the *Lonesome Dove* tradition. No expense has been spared to bring together the finest staff a hunting lodge could hope to assemble. The experience reflects it.

PESTO BAKED SEA BASS

Tomato Cilantro Garnish

1/2 cup diced tomatoes
1 tablespoon chopped fresh cilantro
1 tablespoon olive oil
 Salt and pepper to taste

Cilantro Tomatillo Sauce

1 cup cilantro leaves
1 garlic clove
1/4 cup whole walnuts
1 medium tomatillo, chopped
 Juice of 1 lime
1/3 cup olive oil
 Salt and pepper to taste
2 tablespoons heavy cream
2 tablespoons chicken stock

Leeks

 Vegetable oil
1 cup julienned leeks (thoroughly washed)

Fish

8 ounces Chilean sea bass
3 tablespoons olive oil
2 garlic cloves, chopped
 Salt and pepper to taste

For the garnish, in a bowl mix the tomatoes, cilantro, oil, and salt and pepper together. Set aside.

For the sauce, place the cilantro, garlic, walnuts, tomatillo, lime, olive oil, and salt and pepper in a food processor and process until blended.

Place the sauce in a medium saucepan and add the heavy cream and chicken stock. Stir and heat thoroughly. Cover and keep warm while cooking the fish.

For the leeks, heat the vegetable oil in a deep fryer and fry the leeks until crisp and brown. Place the leeks on a paper towel and set aside.

For the fish, preheat the oven to 375°. Heat the olive oil in an ovenproof pan over medium heat. Sauté the fish in the oil and garlic until brown and crisp, approximately 4 minutes each side. Place the pan in the oven and cook for about 15 minutes. The fish should be moist and tender. Season the fish with salt and pepper to taste.

To serve, place the leeks on a plate. Top with the fish and pour the sauce around the fish. Garnish with the Tomato Cilantro Garnish.

Makes 3 servings.

DOS ANGELES RANCH CRAB AND CORN SOUP

4 ears corn
2 tablespoons butter
1 cup diced white onions
1 cup diced celery
1 bay leaf
1/2 teaspoon thyme
1/2 teaspoon basil
1/2 cup flour
1 cup chicken stock
2 1/2 cups heavy whipping cream
Salt and pepper to taste
1/2 pound crabmeat

Heat the grill to medium–high. Peel the husks back on the corn, remove the silk, and cover the cobs with the husks. Grill the ears of corn for 15 to 20 minutes and then remove them from the heat.

In a medium pot melt the butter. Add the onions, celery, bay leaf, thyme, and basil and sauté for 4 minutes. Cut the corn off the cob, and add the corn kernels to the pot. Let cook for 3 minutes. Add the flour and chicken stock, stirring to remove any lumps, and cook for 4 minutes. Add the cream, salt, and pepper, stirring thoroughly. Simmer on medium to low heat for about 5 minutes. Stir in the crabmeat and heat thoroughly.

Garnish appropriately.

Makes 6 servings.

CRÈME BRULÉE

2 1/2 cups heavy whipping cream
1/2 cup milk
1/4 cup sugar
3 egg yolks
4 whole eggs
1 teaspoon vanilla extract
6 prickly pears, seeded, sliced, and sprinkled with sugar
Brown sugar as desired

Preheat the oven to 300°. Heat the cream, milk, and sugar in a medium saucepan over low heat until almost boiling.

In a separate bowl combine the egg yolks and whole eggs and whisk together. Slowly add the egg mixture to the hot cream while whisking constantly. Continue cooking over low heat, mixing with a wooden spoon until the mixture coats the back of the spoon. Stir in the vanilla.

Pour the mixture evenly into 6 small ovenproof ramekins. Place 1 prickly pear into each dish. Place the dishes into a shallow pan of hot water and bake until firm, about 30 minutes. Cool and then refrigerate for at least 1 hour.

Sprinkle the tops with brown sugar and place under a broiler until the sugar melts, being careful not to burn. Cool again and return to the refrigerator until set.

Makes 6 servings.

LEGACY RANCH
Foreman, Arkansas

For the duck hunter there is only one ultimate destination, and that is Arkansas. Sitting alongside the Mississippi flyway, Arkansas is home to the greatest population of wintering waterfowl in the world. It is the mountaintop that at one time or another duck hunters must visit.

Legacy is in the southwestern corner of Arkansas with more than 3,000 acres of prime Red River bottomland, the low land that borders the river and is extraordinarily fertile and rich due to the river's flooding and the deposition of nutrients over the years. What this means to the hunter is an abundance of wildlife unlike any other topographic area. Where there is water, there is wildlife.

One of the great features of this particular piece of bottomland is the beautiful "river benches." Created by the rise and fall of the river during floods, the benches are alive with lush native grasses, mixed with cottonwood and willow trees. In these benches, wildfowl and upland birds thrive in great numbers, resulting in an unparalleled duck and upland bird hunting experience.

Legacy Ranch is the dream of the Ashley family who for the past ten years have worked to develop a world-class facility for the wing shooter. The 6,000-square-foot lodge is designed to cater to the every need of the twelve guests, and after a day in the field there is nothing better than good southern cooking.

Not only are there ducks by the thousands, but the upland hunter can enjoy a day in the field in pursuit of pheasant or quail with his own dog or with one of the marvelous dogs the ranch provides. Perhaps what creates such fanaticism in bird hunters is the opportunity to spend a day in the field with a great dog. There is no purer relationship than that of man and dog in the field. Only in the field, looking in the eyes of a great hunting dog, can a hunter find honesty, courage, and trust in its purest form.

Legacy Ranch is where all of this takes place, in one of the great natural habitats in North America, hosted by a family whose only desire is to please its guests. It is in this environment that the great sporting tradition of wing shooting is practiced at its highest level.

ARTICHOKE DIP

1   14-ounce can chopped artichoke hearts
1   cup mayonnaise
1   cup grated Parmesan cheese
1/8 teaspoon garlic powder
1   cup mozzarella cheese
     Paprika

Preheat the oven to 350°. Mix the artichokes, mayonnaise, Parmesan, and garlic power in an ovenproof dish. Sprinkle the mixture with the mozzarella cheese and paprika and bake for 25 minutes.

Makes 6 to 8 servings.

HUSH PUPPIES

1   cup flour
1   cup cornmeal
4   teaspoons baking powder
1/4 cup sugar
1   teaspoon salt
1/2 cup chopped onion
1/2 to 3/4 cup buttermilk
     Vegetable oil for frying

In a large bowl combine the flour, cornmeal, baking powder, sugar, and salt. Add the onion and buttermilk. Stir until the batter is just moistened, adding additional buttermilk if needed. In a deep frying pan heat the oil on high. Drop the batter by spoonfuls into the hot oil so the batter is completely covered and can roll in the oil. Cook until brown.

Makes 6 servings.

RUM CAKE

Cake

1   cup chopped pecans
1   18-ounce package yellow cake mix
1   1-ounce package instant vanilla pudding mix
1/2 cup cold water
1/2 cup Bacardi dark rum
4   eggs
1/2 cup vegetable oil

Glaze

1   stick butter
1   cup sugar
1/4 cup water
1/2 cup rum

For the cake, preheat the oven to 325°. Grease a 10-inch tube pan. Sprinkle the pecans onto the bottom of the pan. In a large bowl combine the cake mix, pudding mix, water, rum, eggs, and oil. Beat for 2 minutes until smooth. Pour the cake batter over the pecans. Bake for 1 hour or until a knife inserted in the center comes out clean. Let cool before glazing.

For the glaze, in a medium saucepan melt the butter. Stir in the sugar and water and boil for 5 minutes, stirring constantly. Stir in the rum.

To serve, prick the top of the cake several times with a toothpick and drizzle the glaze over the cake.

Makes 10 servings.

PAUL NELSON FARM

Onida, South Dakota

South Dakota has been the epicenter of pheasant hunting since the introduction of the bright Asian game bird more than 100 years ago. During the fall, over 100,000 pheasant hunters are in the field on opening day. It has become a ritual of sorts for upland hunters, from the wealthiest, who fly in for the event, to the yeomen who drive across the country in campers and pickups for the great hunt.

Paul Nelson, a pioneer in commercial hunting operations in South Dakota, has witnessed this for sixty years. Times were not always good for the pheasant, and the switch from cowboys to farmers destroyed much of the natural habitat needed for good populations. Nelson was one of the first to change agricultural practices on his 10,000 acres to address the needs of the bird, as well as setting aside almost one quarter of his land in the Conservation Reserve Program to provide natural cover and habitat.

The result has been dramatic, and now the pheasant populations are strong. On the Paul Nelson Farm they are nothing short of stunning. On a good day, hunters walking the fields of the farm will put up 200 to 400 wild birds that fly with the speed and determination that only wild birds can offer. It is a hunting experience that has built a reputation as one of the best in the country and brings in those who can afford the best. The Paul Nelson Farm has been jokingly called the "Camp David of the west," a testament to the experience. When hunting with Paul Nelson you are hunting with a man whose life has been devoted to the sport and to the bird;, who knows the pheasant as well as any man alive, and who loves to share his passion with his guests.

The Wall Street Journal's Michael Pearce said in a February, 1996, article, "But there is no time for total relaxation when taken afield by Mr. Nelson's guides and dogs. Proof that agriculture and wildlife can coexist, Paul Nelson's farm's thousands of acres spew birds like bees from a shaken hive. The wingshooting is indeed so good Mr. Nelson had to seek special regulation that allows gunners to take more than the state-regulated three-bird-per-day limit."

When the day is done one retreats to a lodge dedicated to the hunt with every amenity a hunter could desire, from a gun room to kennels to take care of the most important hunters. Here you can enjoy the company of other hunters or find solitude. The food is local, and hunters will eat pheasant like they've never tasted and enjoy the fruits of South Dakota's cattle ranchers.

"Our goal has always been to make you feel right at home," says Nelson. "We're perfect for people who love a great hunt but don't really want to rough it." For any hunter who has walked miles in search of a few pheasant out of pure love for the sport, this is not roughing it. This is paradise.

JESSIE'S MEATLOAF

Topping

1/4   cup ketchup

3   tablespoons brown sugar

1/4   teaspoon nutmeg

1   teaspoon dry mustard

Meatloaf

2   eggs

1/2   cup chopped onion

2   slices bread, torn into small pieces

1/2   8-ounce can tomato sauce

1 1/2   teaspoons salt

1/4   teaspoon freshly ground pepper

2   pounds ground beef

For the topping, combine the ketchup, brown sugar, nutmeg, and dry mustard in a bowl. Set aside.

For the meatloaf, preheat the oven to 350°. Combine the eggs, onion, bread, tomato sauce, salt, and pepper in a large bowl and mix well. Add the ground beef and combine. Shape into a loaf. Spread the topping over the meatloaf. Bake for 1 hour and 15 minutes. Let sit for 15 minutes before serving.

Makes 4 to 6 servings.

PAUL NELSON FARM WILD RICE

2	8-ounce packages wild rice
1	cup chopped onion
2	cups chopped celery
1/2	cup green bell pepper
1	pound mushrooms, sliced
4	tablespoons (1/2 stick) butter
1	20-ounce can cream of mushroom soup
1	20-ounce can cream of chicken soup
1	15-ounce jar Cheez Whiz
1	cup browned bacon

Cook the wild rice according to the package directions, substituting chicken broth for the water. Set aside.

In a large saucepan melt the butter. Add the onion, celery, green pepper, and mushrooms and sauté until translucent. Add the cream of mushroom soup, the cream of chicken soup, and Cheez Whiz.

Pour the rice mixture into a chaffing dish or crockpot and cook for 2 hours at 350°.

Makes 10 servings.

BREAD PUDDING WITH BUTTER SAUCE

Bread Pudding

10	cups torn bread
1/2	to 1 cup raisins (as desired)
1	cup sugar
6	eggs
2	tablespoons vanilla
	Pinch of salt
1	tablespoon cinnamon
4	cups milk
2	tablespoons softened butter

Butter Sauce

1	cup sugar
1/2	cup butter
1/2	cup whipping cream
1 1/2	teaspoons vanilla or 2 teaspoons butterscotch schnapps

For the bread pudding, preheat the oven to 325°. Spray a 13x9-inch pan with nonstick spray. Put the torn bread in the pan and sprinkle with the raisins. In a large bowl combine the sugar, eggs, vanilla, salt, cinnamon, milk, and butter. Mix well and pour over the bread. Push the raisins down into the mixture and let the liquid absorb. Bake for 1 to 1 1/2 hours.

For the sauce, heat the sugar, butter, cream, and vanilla in a medium saucepan over medium heat. Do not boil. Beat for 5 minutes with a spoon.

To serve, pour the sauce over the slices of bread pudding.

Makes 8 servings.

Northeast
THE GREAT NORTH WOODS

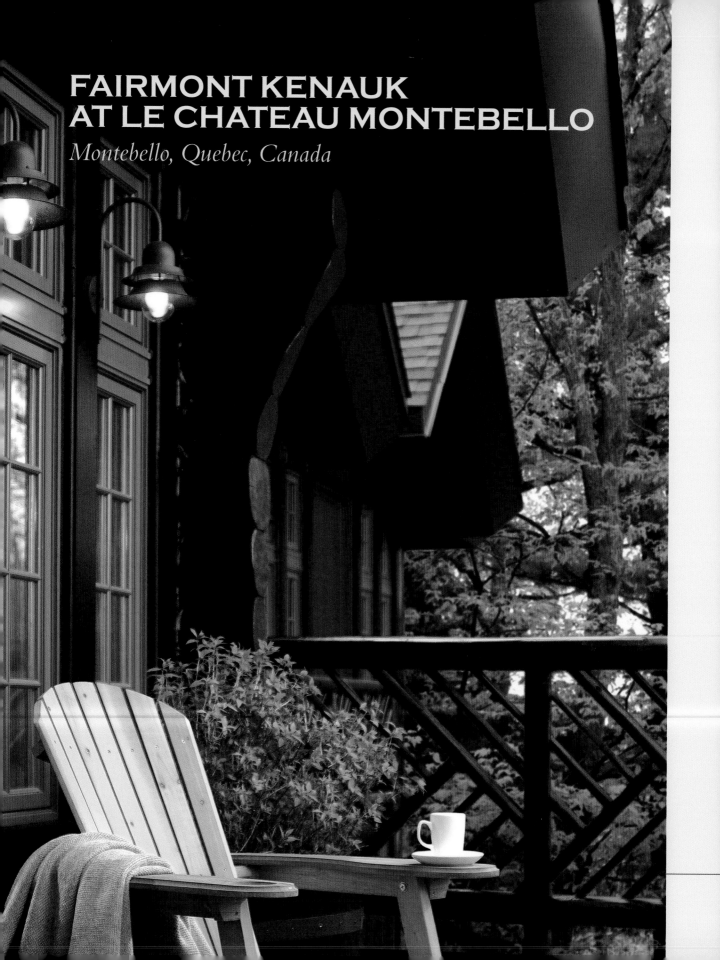

FAIRMONT KENAUK
AT LE CHATEAU MONTEBELLO

Montebello, Quebec, Canada

E very sportsman dreams of a secluded cabin tucked away on a lake or river full of fish, surrounded by thousands of unspoiled wilderness acres; a place of solitude where man and his penchant for development have yet to desecrate the landscape.

The great Canadian north woods that stretch from the Atlantic seacoast to the Great Lakes was at first Algonquin land. Samuel de Champlain first met the Algonquin in 1603 and their long association in the fur trade began. In a region halfway between Montreal and Ottawa, the king of France granted what is now known as Kenauk to Quebec's first bishop, Monseigneur Laval. "Reserve de la Petite Nation," as it was called then, was a 100-square-mile, 65,000-acre protected wilderness domain.

Today Kenauk is part of the Fairmont Le Chateau Montebello, a historic luxury resort with a legendary red cedar log building that has welcomed guests from around the world since 1930. The resort is magnificent unto itself, but it is the wilderness cottages on the lakes of the preserve that set this experience apart. Thirteen beautifully maintained cabins sit on the shores of seventy lakes and ponds within the borders of the preserve; eight of the cabins are the only structure on their respective lakes.

When a guest enters the gates of Kenauk Preserve it may be many miles to reach one of the cabins. Everything a sportsman could want is provided, right down to the boats at the dock. To rise in the morning and set out in a kayak across a Canadian lake, knowing you will not see another human, is something rare indeed these days. Because of this lack of human incursion, the wildlife is extraordinary and the fishing is world-class. There are no gasoline engines on the lakes, no noise but the call of a loon or the howl of a coyote. If the need arises for social interaction or a

meal equivalent to the best that Europe has to offer, then a short drive from the preserve is the Fairmont Chateau de Montebello, one of the most famous of the grand Canadian resort hotels and its restaurant, Aux Chantignoles. Here is the very best of both worlds: complete wilderness solitude, coupled with a world-class resort and cuisine. For the sportsman, the dream of a wilderness cabin experience can be unquestionably realized—a cabin of your own, a lake of your own, and only the loons for company.

DEER MEDALLIONS FROM BOILEAU

White Bean Purée

1	cup dried white beans
1/4	cup mirepoix (combination of diced onions, leek, carrots, and garlic)
5	cups chicken broth
1/4	cup cream

Roasted Vegetables

1/4	cup diced yellow turnip
1/4	cup diced carrot
1/4	cup diced celeriac root
1/4	cup diced butternut squash
1/4	cup diced yellow beet
2	tablespoons unsalted butter
1/4	cup apple juice

Wild Elderberry Sauce

1/4	cup red wine
2	tablespoons minced shallots
1	cup game stock or beef stock
2	tablespoons elderberries
	Salt and pepper to taste

Deer Medallions

1 1/2	pounds deer loin
	Salt and pepper to taste
2	tablespoons vegetable oil
	Wild elderberries for garnish

For the white bean purée, soak the white beans in water overnight. Drain the beans. Combine the beans and the mirepoix in a large saucepan with the broth. Bring to a boil. Reduce the heat and cook until tender over medium heat. Purée the beans in a blender. Return to the saucepan and stir in the cream.

For the roasted vegetables, preheat the oven to 350°. Place the turnip, carrots, celeriac root, butternut squash, and yellow beets on a baking sheet with sides. Add the butter and apple juice over the vegetables and bake until golden brown, about 30 minutes.

For the sauce, in a medium saucepan add the wine and shallots. Bring to a boil over medium-high heat and cook until reduced by half. Add the stock and elderberries. Bring to boil and reduce until the desired consistency. Add salt and pepper and strain the sauce through a fine strainer.

For the deer medallions, sprinkle the deer with salt and pepper. Heat the oil in 14-inch ovenproof skillet over medium-high heat. Sear the deer loin in the oil until brown, about 4 minutes on each side. Place the skillet in the oven. Roast until a thermometer inserted into the center registers 130° to 135°, about 12 minutes. Transfer the roast to a platter and tent with foil. Let stand 10 minutes before slicing into medallions.

To serve, place white bean purée in the center of each plate and set a medallion on top. Place roasted vegetables around the medallion. Add a ribbon of sauce and wild elderberries as garnish.

Makes 4 servings.

SMOKED TROUT TARTARE AND GOAT CHEESE

8   ounces smoked trout
5   ounces fresh goat cheese
1/2 cup heavy cream
1   teaspoon chopped fresh chives
     Salt and pepper to taste
4   sheets of brik or phyllo dough
2   tablespoons melted butter
1/2 cucumber
     Radishes and lettuce leaves for garnish, if
     desired

Preheat the oven to 300°. Finely dice two-thirds of the smoked trout. In a bowl mix the diced trout, the goat cheese, cream, chives, and salt and pepper to taste.

Spread a sheet of brik or phyllo dough on a damp towel with the narrow end toward you. Brush with melted butter. Carefully shape one sheet of phyllo dough inside each of 4 individual muffin cups. Bake until golden.

Using a vegetable peeler, peel thin ribbons of cucumber and place inside the phyllo cups in a circle. Spoon the cheese mixture into the cup. Place 3 slices of smoked trout on a plate, add the phyllo cup on the side. Garnish with radishes and lettuce leaves, if desired.

Makes 4 servings.

BONSECOURS ORCHARD APPLE AND MAPLE TATIN

Honey Ice Cream
5   egg yolks
1/2 cup honey
1   cup heavy cream
1   cup milk

Tatin
1/2 17-ounce package puff pastry (1 puff pastry
     sheet)
1 1/2 cups maple syrup
4   Granny Smith apples, peeled, cored and
     quartered,

For the ice cream, combine the egg yolks and honey in a casserole dish. Heat the cream and milk in a medium saucepan over medium heat. When almost boiling, remove from the heat and pour gently into the egg and honey mixture. Stir well and cook until it reaches 185°. Transfer to an ice cream machine and follow the manufacturer's instructions.

For the tatin, roll the puff pastry sheet on a floured work surface with a floured rolling pin to 1/4 inch thick. Brush off excess flour. Cut out one 10-inch round or four 4-inch rounds with a sharp knife, using a plate or bowl as a guide. Transfer the round or rounds to a baking sheet and chill.

Preheat the oven to 350°. In a small saucepan cook the maple syrup over moderately high heat, stirring frequently until thickened. Pour the syrup into a 10-inch mold or four 4-inch molds. Let cool and place the apples on top. Drape the pastry round over the apples, tucking the edge around them. Cut a few holes in the top to allow steam to escape. Bake for 20 minutes, or until the pastry is golden brown.

Loosen the edges of the pastry with a knife. Invert onto a platter quickly and carefully. Rearrange any apples that may have fallen out. Serve warm with the Honey Ice Cream.

Makes 4 servings.

GLENDORN
Bradford, Pennsylvania

There are lodges that are created from a vision of a remote and wonderful place. There are lodges that are created because of a specific activity such as hunting or fishing. And there are the few lodges that have evolved out the experience of years in a place that is revered by the owners. Glendorn is one of these places.

Built in the 1920s by C. G. Dorn for his family, Glendorn has been a retreat for six generations—a place where this close-knit family gathered and created traditions. Dorn and his son Forest discovered a method to extract oil from depleted oil fields and built a significant fortune. An avid outdoorsman, Dorn decided his family needed a place to pursue their outdoor interests, and Glendorn was born.

The estate lies on 1,280 acres of pristine eastern hardwood forest in the northwest corner of Pennsylvania in the Allegheny Mountains, close to some of the best eastern fly fishing there is. Dorn was an ardent angler and the rivers, streams, and lakes in and around Glendorn were his favorites. Today they are offered to Glendorn guests with the services of Orvis-endorsed guides who take anglers from classic small stream and stillwater fishing, to float trips on the Allegheny and Clarion rivers. The steelhead fishing in the fall and winter is spectacular and Perk Perkins, CEO of Orvis, has called it one of the best steelhead experiences he has had.

Visitors can stay in the main house or one of the twelve cottages around the estate. One can choose to be social or secluded, but in every case, you feel as if you are a member of the Dorn family.

A member of Relais & Châteaux, one of the most prestigious collections of destinations worldwide, Glendorn offers exquisite dining under the direction of chefs Charles and Colleen Zeran. Their eclectic cuisine is best described as neo-global, combining flavors, ingredients, and styles from around the world, as well as a few techniques of their own, to create daily menus that are unique in taste and presentation, and often as thought-provoking as they are delicious.

Charles also manages the wine program and has assembled a *Wine Spectator* Award-winning cellar, allowing for the integrated celebration of food and wine. The wine list includes selections from eleven different countries on five continents and wines from all major regions and grape varietals. Every evening, Charles pairs each course of the five-course menu with a different wine from around the world.

The Dorn family has loved and cared for Glendorn for eighty years, and now they've opened their beloved estate for others to enjoy. It is as unique as it is beautiful and guests immediately feel as if they are members of this wonderful family.

CAMEMBERT HALIBUT GRATINÉE

2   whole lobsters
1   cup diced carrots
1   cup diced yellow onion
1   cup diced celery
2   bay leaves
1/2 teaspoon black peppercorns
1   quart heavy cream
1/4 cup dry sherry
1/2 cup brandy
    Salt
    Cayenne pepper
1   pound halibut fillet, cut into four 4-ounce portions
    Black pepper
    Vegetable oil
16 asparagus spears, blanched
    Butter
1/2 pound Camembert cheese, rind removed and sliced into 4 slices

Steam or boil the lobsters. Remove the meat from the claws and reserve the tails for another use.

Place the lobster shells, carrots, onion, celery, bay leaves, and peppercorns in a stockpot with about 1 gallon of water. Bring to a boil and reduce to about 2 cups. Strain the stock into another pot and reduce to about 1/2 cup. Add the cream, sherry, and brandy and reduce to about 2 cups. Season to taste with salt and cayenne. Strain. Keep warm.

Preheat the oven to 400°. Season the halibut with salt and black pepper. Lightly brown on both sides in a hot sauté pan with a small amount of vegetable oil. Remove and place on a baking sheet and bake for about 4 to 5 minutes depending on the thickness of the fish.

In a sauté pan warm the asparagus and lobster claws in a small amount of butter. Bring the lobster sauce to a boil.

Remove the halibut from oven. Top each piece with Camembert and return to oven for 1 minute.

Divide the asparagus between four warm plates. Place the halibut on top of the asparagus and a lobster claw on top of each piece of fish. Froth up the lobster sauce with an immersion blender or cappuccino frother. Spoon just the froth on top of the fish. Re-froth as necessary to sauce all the plates. Serve immediately.

Note: To steam the lobsters, bring 1 1/2 inches of water to a boil. Add the lobsters and cook them for 15 minutes, covered tightly. To boil the lobsters, bring to a boil enough water to cover the lobsters completely. Add the lobsters and return to a boil. Cook for 12 minutes.

Makes 4 servings.

MACADAMIA CRUSTED FOIE GRAS

2   pints blackberries, divided
1/2 pint blueberries
1   loaf brioche bread
3   eggs
1/2 cup half-and-half
1/4 teaspoon cayenne pepper
1/2 teaspoon salt
1   vanilla bean, seeds scraped (or 1 teaspoon vanilla extract)
     Butter
12   ounces grade A duck foie gras, cut into 4 3-ounce slices
1/2 cup roasted crushed macadamia nuts

Purée 1 pint of the blackberries. Strain and place in a sauté pan over medium heat. When warm, add the remaining pint blackberries and the blueberries. Remove from the heat and cover to keep warm.

Remove the crust from the brioche and slice into 1/2-inch-thick slices. Combine the eggs, half-and-half, cayenne, salt, and vanilla bean seeds or vanilla extract in a shallow dish. Soak the bread in the mixture for about 1 minute.

Lightly butter a large skillet and place the bread into the pan over medium-high heat. Brown on both sides. Remove to a warm oven.

Heat another sauté pan until very hot. Season the foie gras slices with salt and pepper. Cook for about 90 seconds on each side.

Place a slice of the French toast in the center of 4 plates. Top with a slice of foie gras. Lightly cover the foie gras with the crushed macadamia nuts. Spoon the warm berries and sauce around the French toast.

Makes 4 servings.

RHUBARB AND STRAWBERRY NAPOLEONS WITH VANILLA MASCARPONE

Napoleons

1 1/2 cups plus 2 tablespoons sugar, divided

2   cups water

8 to 10 rhubarb stalks

1   1-pound package phyllo dough, thawed
      Melted butter
      Sugar for sprinkling

1   cup rhubarb juice

1   cup strawberry juice

3/4   cup heavy cream

1   tablespoon finely chopped ginger

1   vanilla bean, split lengthwise

1/2   cup mascarpone

4   strawberries, quartered

Mint Syrup

1   cup water

1   cup sugar

2   cups chopped fresh mint

For the Napoleons, preheat the oven to 250°. Combine 1 cup of the sugar and the water in a saucepan and heat until the sugar dissolves. Using a vegetable peeler, peel the rhubarb into long strips. Add to the saucepan and cook until tender. Remove the rhubarb strips, reserving the cooking liquid. Place the rhubarb on a nonstick sheet pan and bake for 25 to 30 minutes until golden and almost dry.

Increase the oven temperature to 425°. Lay one sheet of phyllo on a work surface (cover the remaining phyllo with a towel to prevent drying); brush with melted butter and sprinkle with sugar. Repeat the layers three times. Cut into 3-inch squares. Line a sheet pan with parchment paper. Lay the squares on the parchment paper and cover with a second sheet of parchment paper and second sheet pan. Bake until golden brown, about 8 minutes.

Combine the rhubarb, reserving 2 to 3 strips, and strawberry juices with 1/4 to 1/2 cup sugar to taste. Reduce the mixture until you have approximately 1/2 cup liquid.

In a saucepan combine the heavy cream and ginger and heat to a simmer. Remove from the heat and steep for 10 minutes. Strain the liquid into a mixing bowl, adding the seeds from the vanilla bean. Whip until soft peaks form. Add the remaining 2 tablespoons sugar and the mascarpone and whip until completely blended. Set the mixture in the refrigerator until ready to use.

Cut the remaining rhubarb in 1/2 inch pieces and simmer in the reserved poaching liquid until tender. Add the strawberry quarters until just until softened.

For the mint syrup, combine the water and sugar in a saucepan and bring to boil. Add the mint.

Place a phyllo square on a plate and top with a small amount of the mascarpone filling. Top with a small amount of the rhubarb and strawberry compote. Repeat this process twice ending with a phyllo sheet. Take 3 to 4 rhubarb strips and lean them against the Napoleon as garnish. Drizzle the mint sauce around the plate.

Makes 8 servings.

LIBBY CAMPS
Millinocket Lake, Maine

The mention of Maine instantly evokes an image of water. Whether crashing against the rocks of Maine's coastline or coursing through the endless rivers, streams, ponds, and lakes of Maine's great north woods, water is the lifeblood of Maine and its history.

The Libby Camps in the forests of Aroostook County have lived off the water and its offerings for more than one hundred years. Catering to the angling desires of men and women through four generations, the storied history of the camps is the stuff of Maine legend. The camps today are where legend and fact meet and the true Maine fishing experience can be found.

Since 1977 Matt and Ellen Libby have been running the camps, which have access to an extraordinary range of remote lakes, ponds, and streams. There are eight cabins at the main camp on Millinocket Lake. There are ten more camps spread across the waters of northern Maine and a set of camps called RiverKeep Lodge in Labrador.

The Libbys are fishermen, and while anyone is welcomed with open arms, the Libbys cater to the angler, offering access to wild trout and salmon rivers, ponds, and lakes that otherwise would be virtually inaccessible. Using two floatplanes and more than ten guides, the entire north woods experience is open to Libby Camps guests. Perhaps most important is the opportunity to catch the great American brook trout in its native waters.

Each private log cabin faces the lake with a big bay window. The cabins are heated with woodstoves, lit only with kerosene lanterns,

and are comfortably appointed. They are connected to the main lodge by trails through the woods. It is at the main lodge that Ellen Libby creates the meals that, combined with the extraordinary fishing, keep her guests coming back year after year.

The cooks of Libby Camps have been making guests feel at home since Melissa Trafton Libby began cooking at a hotel in Oxbow in 1880. This was the only lodging at the headwaters of the Aroostook, and Melissa Libby became a legend in her own right to the sportsmen of Maine. Matt's mother, Elsie Parker Libby, was the third generation and many of the recipes that grace the Libby Camps' tables come from

her. In 1976 Elsie sold the camps to Matt and his new wife. Ellen Curry Libby now carries on the tradition of the Libby Camps' tables. Her recipes, combined with those of the former great Libby cooks, have forged a tradition of great table fare that simply adds to the Libby legend and the great northern Maine wilderness experience.

ROAST BEEF AT LIBBY'S

Libby's is known for its family-style cooking and for great roast beef any way its customers like. It is an annual favorite of the guests. If you want your roast beef perfect each and every time—rare in the middle and medium toward the outside—here is the recipe for you.

1 boneless top round
Seasoning to taste, such as Italian seasoning and garlic pepper

Preheat the oven to 500°. Place the roast in the oven and cook at 500° for 5 minutes per pound (3 pounds = 15 minutes, 5 pounds = 25 minutes). Do not exceed 30 minutes at 500°.

Reduce the heat to about 180°. Let the roast cook for at least 2 hours. It is very important that you do not open the oven door!

You can enjoy your roast anytime, leaving it in the oven on warm until ready to serve, for up to 2 hours. It will always be rare, juicy, and tender.

Makes 10 servings.

EDYE'S WHOLE WHEAT BISCUITS

2 cups all-purpose flour
1 cup whole wheat flour
2 tablespoons sugar
4 1/2 teaspoons baking powder
1/2 teaspoon salt
3/4 teaspoon cream of tartar
3/4 cup (1 1/2 sticks) cold butter, chopped
1 egg
1 1/4 cup whole milk

Preheat the oven to 450°. In a large bowl combine all-purpose flour, whole wheat flour, sugar, bak-ing powder, salt, and cream of tartar. Add the cold butter and mix well with a pastry blender. Add the egg and milk and mix until just moistened. Turn the dough onto a floured surface. Knead for 10 to 15 times. Roll out to 1 inch thick. Cut with a biscuit cutter and place on a greased baking pan. Bake for 10 to 15 minutes.

Makes 12 to 15 biscuits.

AROOSTOOK FIDDLEHEAD SALAD

Fiddleheads are available fresh in Maine in mid-May and can be frozen or canned. They are also available commercially, canned by a small company called Belle of Maine. The fiddlehead is the young shoot of the ostrich fern, which grows along floodplains near streams and rivers throughout Maine. They are also excellent as a steamed veggie.

Dressing

2 tablespoons wine vinegar
6 tablespoons olive oil
1 garlic clove, minced
1/2 teaspoon Dijon mustard
1/2 teaspoon paprika
1 teaspoon dried chives
1/2 teaspoon ground black pepper

Salad

2 cups cooked fiddleheads
2 hard-boiled eggs, chopped

For the dressing, combine the vinegar, oil, garlic, mustard, paprika, chives, and pepper. Whisk well to emulsify the oil and vinegar.

For the salad, put the fiddleheads in a large bowl. Pour the dressing over them and sprinkle the eggs over top.

Makes 4 servings.

BLUEBERRY COBBLER

1   tablespoon butter
2   cups fresh or frozen blueberries
1/2 teaspoon cinnamon
1   tablespoon lemon juice
3/4 cup sugar
1   cup all-purpose flour
1/4 teaspoon salt
3   tablespoons butter
1   teaspoon baking powder
1/2 cup milk
1   tablespoon cornstarch
1   cup sugar
    Dash of salt
1   cup boiling water

Preheat the oven to 375°. Grease the inside of an 8x8-inch loaf pan with 1 tablespoon of butter. Place the blueberries in the pan, sprinkle with cinnamon and lemon juice. Mix together the sugar, all-purpose flour, salt, butter, baking powder, and milk, making a batter. Spread the batter over the blueberries.

Combine the cornstarch, sugar, and salt. Mix well and sprinkle over the batter. Pour the boiling water over the entire mixture. Place in the oven and bake at 375° for 1 hour. Serve warm with whipped cream or ice cream.

Note: Raspberries may be substituted for the blueberries, or you can use a mixture of both blueberries and raspberries. A double recipe fits in a 13x9-inch pan.

Makes 8 to 12 servings.

NEMACOLIN
WOODLANDS RESORT

Farmington, Pennsylvania

The image of a hunting and fishing lodge is generally one of a log building in the wilderness surrounded by mountains and lakes with little else to do but hunt and fish. But Nemacolin Woodlands Resort is different. While the fishing is as good as Eastern fly fishing can be and the waters of southwest Pennsylvania are loaded with trout, Nemacolin is a true family resort with something for everyone.

Anyone who has spent time in the Appalachian chain can easily understand the beauty of the Laurel Highlands region in the southwest corner of Pennsylvania, where the Keystone State tucks itself into the corner of West Virginia. Set on 3,000 acres, Nemacolin offers a staggering number of activities including golf, off-road driving, fishing, shooting, wildlife viewing, skiing, and even a beach and marina. There are stores, art galleries, a 200-seat lecture hall, meeting facilities, and an airstrip. The list of activities is more than enough to keep a very large family busy every hour of every day. There are archery ranges, ropes courses, biking, tennis, and an equestrian center.

It is no wonder that dining is such a large part of the Nemocolin experience. Two of the numerous restaurants are 4-Diamond rated. Lautrec, in the Chateau LaFayette, is Nemacolin's most acclaimed restaurant, the "Grande Dame" of fine dining in western Pennsylvania. The Aqueous is an upscale steakhouse with a menu focused on locally-raised beef, lamb, pork, and chicken created with progressive thought, set against the harmony of the natural surroundings of the Laurel Highlands and inspired by the architecture of Frank Lloyd Wright's Falling Waters. The cuisine and décor of other taverns and restaurants are equally enjoyable, if not quite as formal.

Nemacolin Woodlands Resort is also home to the largest wine cellar in the state of Pennsylvania. With a capacity of more than 17,000 bottles, the cellar is an amazing study of wines from around

the world. Nemacolin's resident Sommelier Brian Henderson invites guests for a tasting of world-class wines from around the globe in the Academie du Vin.

But as busy as this sounds, there is escape. The surrounding countryside is beautiful, and the waters of Nemacolin offer quiet solitude for the angler in the mountain streams and rivers surrounding the resort. For hunters, the Shooting Academy where they can hone their shooting skills is four miles from the resort and spread across a 140-acre complex. It features thirty sporting clays shooting stations, European pheasant flush fields, towers, fun stations, and five stand pavilions.

Nemacolin is not your ordinary hunting or fishing lodge by any means, but it does offer hunters and anglers the chance to do what they love most while the rest of the family is having a wonderful time as well. It is the best of all worlds.

FARFALLE WITH ROCK SHRIMP

Mayonnaise

Zest of 2 lemons
Juice of 1 lemon
1   cup mayonnaise
1   tablespoon sugar
2   tablespoons minced parsley
1/2 teaspoon Cajun seasoning
1/4 cup grated Parmesan
Salt and pepper to taste

Farfalle

1/4 cup (1/2 stick) butter
1   teaspoon minced garlic
8   ounces rock shrimp (approximately 2 cups)
8   ounces uncooked farfalle pasta
1/2 cup julienned red bell pepper
1/2 cup julienned red onion

For the mayonnaise, in a bowl combine the lemon zest, lemon juice, mayonnaise, sugar, parsley, Cajun seasoning, Parmesan, and salt and pepper to taste. Mix thoroughly.

For the farfalle, melt the butter in a sauté pan. Add the minced garlic and sauté until golden. Place the rock shrimp in the pan and sauté until cooked through. Place the shrimp in a bowl and refrigerate to chill.

Cook the pasta in boiling salted water until *al dente*, about 8 minutes. Immediately drain the pasta. Submerge the pasta in ice water until completely chilled. Remove the pasta from the ice water, drain thoroughly, and place in a large bowl. Add the chilled rock shrimp, red pepper, and red onion and toss.

Add the lemon mayonnaise to the farfalle and toss to coat. This should be dressed a bit heavily as the pasta will absorb some dressing as it sits. Season with salt and pepper to taste. Refrigerate overnight.

Makes 8 to 10 servings.

BABY BACK RIBS

Rib Rub

1/2   pound firmly packed brown sugar

4   tablespoons Cajun spice

1 1/2 teaspoons salt

1 1/2 tablespoons black pepper

10   pounds baby back ribs

Rib Boil

4   cups Cattlemen's Classic Barbecue Sauce (or similar)

1   cup Red Hot (or similar cayenne pepper sauce such as Tabasco)

8   cups water

1/4 celery stalk, roughly chopped

1 1/2 jumbo carrots, roughly chopped

1 1/2 jumbo Spanish onions, chopped

Honey Barbecue Sauce

18   cups ketchup

1/2 cup chili sauce

1/2 cup Worcestershire sauce

1   tablespoon liquid smoke

1   cup honey

1/2 cup molasses

2   cups orange juice

1   cup apple cider vinegar

1/2 pound brown sugar

1/2 cup Myers Rum

1/4 cup Dijon mustard

1   cup orange marmalade

2   tablespoons powder

1   tablespoon cumin

1/4 cup chili powder

1 1/2 teaspoons allspice

1   cup small diced onion

For the rib rub, in a large container mix the brown sugar, Cajun spice, salt, and pepper together. Rub the rib rub over the ribs 24 hours before cooking.

Heat a grill to high and sear the ribs on the grill to make grill marks.

For the rib boil, preheat the oven to 350° to 375°. In a large stockpot combine the barbecue sauce, hot sauce, water, celery, carrots, and onions. Arrange the ribs in large pans. Pour the rib boil evenly over the ribs. Cook in the oven until tender, about 3 hours.

While the ribs are cooking, prepare the honey barbecue sauce. In a large container, combine the ketchup, chili sauce, Worcestershire sauce, liquid smoke, honey, molasses, orange juice, vinegar, brown sugar, rum, mustard, marmalade, garlic powder, cumin, chili powder, allspice, and onion.

To serve, remove from the cooking liquid and baste with the Honey Barbecue Sauce.

Makes 10 pounds of ribs.

LOBSTER BISQUE

Lobster Stock

	Vegetable oil
2	pounds cleaned lobsters
2	cups chopped tomatoes
1	garlic bulb, cut in half horizontally
1	bunch tarragon
3	carrots, peeled and sliced
1	bulb fennel, sliced
48	ounces clam juice
1	gallon chicken stock

Lobster Bisque

2	gallons lobster stock
4	quarts heavy cream
6	cups cooked basmati rice

Preheat a large stockpot on the stove until almost smoking. Add oil to the pan and sear the lobsters until bright red. Add the chopped tomato and cook down until dry. Add the garlic, tarragon, carrots, and fennel. Cover with the clam juice and stock.

Simmer for 2 hours. Drain through a coarse strainer and through a fine strainer.

For the bisque, reduce the stock and the cream by half in separate saucepans. Combine the stock and cream into one pan and bring to a simmer. Purée the soup in batches in a blender, 4 cups of soup and 1 cup of rice at a time. Do not fill the blender more than three-quarters full and be sure to cover it with a towel when blending to prevent burning.

Strain the soup through a fine strainer into the saucepan. Reheat it, blend it with a hand blender, and serve.

Makes 1 1/2 gallons.

BUMBLEBERRY PIE

1/4	cup (1/2 stick) butter
2	tablespoons sugar
1	cup rhubarb
2	tablespoons frozen blackberries (juices reserved)
1/4	cup frozen blueberries (juices reserved)
1/4	cup frozen raspberries (juices reserved)
1/4	cup frozen strawberries (juices reserved)
1	tablespoon sugar
1/3	cup cornstarch
2	tablespoons water
2	9-inch piecrusts

In a medium sauté pan melt the butter and add 2 tablespoons sugar and rhubarb. Cook until the rhubarb is tender. Place the berries in a colander resting over a bowl. Pour the rhubarb over the berries. Let the berries and rhubarb drain overnight in the refrigerator, collecting the juices in the bowl.

Preheat the oven to 350°. Place the berries and rhubarb in a separate bowl, and set aside.

In a small saucepan bring the reserved juices to a boil with 1 tablespoon sugar. In a small bowl, combine the cornstarch with the water to make a slurry and add to the boiling juice, stirring until thickened.

Add the thickened juice to the berries and rhubarb. Pour the mixture into a crust-lined pie plate.

Roll out the remaining piecrust into an 11-inch round on the lightly floured surface. Cover the filling with the top crust, pressing the edge to seal. Cut slits in the crust to allow steam to escape.

Bake for 45 minutes or until the crust is browned and the apple is cooked.

Makes one 9-inch pie.

TROUT IN PAPER
WITH RICOTTA GNOCCHI

Ricotta Gnocchi

2   cups ricotta cheese

2   egg yolks

1 1/2 cups flour

1   teaspoon dried chives

1   teaspoon dried parsley

1   teaspoon dried basil

1   tablespoon olive oil

      Salt and pepper to taste

Trout

4   pieces broccolini

      Salt and pepper

1   8-ounce trout fillet

2   ounces lump crabmeat

2   cups (4 sticks) butter, cut into pieces

1/2   cup chopped Kalamata olives

2   tablespoons orange zest

2   teaspoons chopped fresh chervil

2   teaspoons chopped fresh parsley

2   teaspoons chopped fresh chives

For the gnocchi, set a colander lined with cheese-cloth over a large bowl. Place the ricotta in the prepared strainer; cover with plastic wrap and refrigerate overnight.

Place the drained ricotta cheese into a large mixing bowl. Add the egg yolks and mix together. Slowly add the flour to the mixture until completely incorporated. Add the chives, parsley, basil, olive oil, and season with salt and pepper.

Roll out the dough into 1/2-inch-wide pieces. Cut to desired size and shape. Drop the gnocchi into boiling water for 2 minutes or until they begin to float; drain.

For the trout, preheat the oven to 350°. Cut parchment paper large enough to form a packet around the trout. Place the parchment paper on a baking sheet. Place the broccolini pieces in the center of the parchment and season with salt and pepper. Top with the trout, crabmeat, butter, olives, orange zest, chervil, parsley, and chives. Wrap the parchment paper over to cover the trout and fold the ends to form a packet.

Bake for 6 to 7 minutes. To serve, cut the parchment paper and serve with the Ricotta Gnocchi.

Makes 3 servings.

THE ROD AND GUN CLUB
AT POCONO MANOR
Pocono Manor, Pennsylvania

In the late nineteenth century as the populations of New York and Philadelphia burgeoned and the cities grew congested and dirty from the industrial revolution, the wealthy began to seek enclaves of beauty and respite in the nearby mountains of the Catskills to the north and the Poconos to the west. Grand resorts began to spring up on great tracts of land. Families moved to these resorts for long periods of time, and the list of outdoor activities was endless. They were like land-based cruise ships, totally self-contained, catering to the whims of everyone from the children to the grandparents, with expansive dining rooms and family tables, huge libraries, and massive fireplaces that heated great halls filled with leather chairs and game tables.

In the Poconos the big three were Buck Hill, Skytop, and Pocono Manor. Grand private cottages began to surround the hotels as large families desired more privacy but still wanted all the amenities of the resort. As time changed these grand old ladies fell on hard times. Recently, though, a resurgence of interest has taken place with the desire to bring these grand resorts back to their original splendor. Pocono Manor is in the midst of this great resurgence and is again offering that magnificent nineteenth-century resort experience.

Listed on the National Registry of Historic Places, Pocono Manor is surrounded by 3,500 acres of Appalachian forest with an understory of mountain laurel and rhododendron. Classic eastern brook trout streams run through the property where anglers cast small flies to feisty brookies, surrounded by a canopy of green. It is true eastern close-quarters fishing where stealth and approach are everything. It is the environ where fly fishing as we know it was born.

Recently the Rod and Gun Club at Pocono Manor was reborn, and there is now a world-class sporting clays range, five stand trap, and skeet range where top national events are held regularly. The Rod and Gun Club building was originally one of the prominent old private cottages of a wealthy Philadelphia family that had fallen into disrepair. It is now refurbished into a classic gun club reminiscent of the old hunting clubs of the Hudson Valley—a tribute to what once was, and what still is, desired for the sporting gentleman.

The manor itself is massive with 257 rooms redone in the architecture and furnishings of the manor's golden age. Rooms are appointed with finely crafted mahogany furniture, patterned rugs, and the most spectacular panoramic view of the Pocono Mountains. The main lobby with exquisite fieldstone fireplaces, antique grandfather clocks, paintings, and old world ambiance is comfortable and inviting.

One might think that a place so close to the majority of the U.S. population would be overcrowded, overdeveloped, and designed to cater to the masses, but once through the gates of Pocono Manor, years melt away, old world grandeur appears, and the graciousness of the nineteenth century is once again available to those looking to escape the hurtling pace of the twenty-first century.

MARINATED GRILLED VEGETABLE SALAD

1   large zucchini, sliced lengthwise
1   large yellow squash, sliced lengthwise
1/2   red onion, thickly sliced
1/4   red eggplant, thickly sliced
1/2   red bell pepper, seeded
1/2   green pepper, seeded
1/2   yellow pepper, seeded
2   portobello mushrooms, halved
24   asparagus spears
1   12-ounce bottle balsamic vinaigrette
1   large tomato, diced

Preheat a grill to medium. Toss the zucchini, squash, onion, eggplant, red pepper, green pepper, yellow pepper, mushrooms, and asparagus in the balsamic vinaigrette. Drain the vegetables, reserving the vinaigrette. Grill the vegetables for 2 to 3 minutes until tender. Set aside to cool slightly.

Dice the grilled onion, eggplant, and peppers into 1/2-inch chunks.

Place the asparagus on a plate and top with a ring mold. Place the mushrooms in the mold, followed with the chopped vegetables. Top with the diced tomato. Remove the mold and drizzle the plate with the reserved balsamic vinaigrette.

Makes 4 servings.

CHICKEN CABERNET

8   4-ounce chicken cutlets
    All-purpose flour for dredging
    Salt and pepper
2   tablespoons vegetable oil
1   teaspoon chopped fresh garlic
2   cups assorted mushrooms (crimini, shiitake, oyster)
1/2   cup cabernet wine
1   cup chicken stock

Dredge the chicken in the flour seasoned with salt and pepper. Heat the vegetable oil in a pan and sauté the chicken for 3 minutes per side or until cooked through. Remove the chicken from the pan. Add the garlic and mushrooms and cook until tender. Add the cabernet wine and chicken stock. Reduce by two-thirds to make a nice sauce. Add salt and pepper if needed.

Serve with risotto and sautéed baby carrots.

Makes 8 servings.

WEATHERBY'S
Grand Lake Stream, Maine

Perhaps no other sporting endeavor gives such credence to its history and tradition as fishing. While there are wonderful new fishing lodges, there is a tangible reward in stepping into an old and venerable lodge that has seen over a century of sport fishing in one of the great storied waters of fishing history.

Weatherby's is such a place. Long revered by anglers, Weatherby's sits alongside Grand Lake Stream in northeastern Maine, a three-mile river that connects West Grand Lake and Big Lake, two of the best lakes in the world for pursuing Ounaniche (pronounced Wan-na-neesh), the landlocked salmon of northern Maine. Built in 1870, Weatherby's lodge has changed little from its early days, and the fishing experience is thankfully unchanged as well. Maine guides still take their clients into the lakes in huge cedar rib and plank canoes, locally built and designed to handle the big water of these northern Maine lakes.

Grand Lake Stream has been a fly fishing only river since 1903. It is home to one of the original four strains of landlocked salmon called "leapers" or "shiners," always spectacular adversaries, who have lured sportsmen to these woods since men began telling other men about fishing. One hundred years ago they came from Boston and Portland by whatever means available to pursue these fish. In a 1903 copy of *Maine Sportsman*, one Dr. Augustus C. Hamlin described his experience with his Indian guide Toma.

"Tossing my fly into the air, the breeze bore it along down the stream, and gently and gracefully lowered toward the surface of the water. It had settled to within a foot or two of the stream when a half a dozen salmon whose bright sides glistened in the sunlight like silver, sprang into the air after it. . . . Across the stream the noble fish dashed and sprang into the air shaking himself to get rid of the fatal hook. . . . The game little salmon was soon at my feet and a more beautiful fish I never saw. Twenty-four more casts I made and each time safely landed my fish. Toma's explanation was, as we considered the beautiful fish that I had caught:

'He sea salmon; but he in fresh water, he forgot to go to sea. Big lake his sea. He live in lake.' "

Though one would wish the fishing were still that prolific, Weatherby's is a place where it is as close as an angler could hope in modern times. Ranked the number-two fishing lodge in the United States by *Field and Stream Magazine*, Weatherby's is a lodge that takes its heritage seriously and offers the angler an experience that is essentially unchanged from Dr. Hamlin's. The fifteen individual cabins are rustic and comfortable, each with a fireplace and screened porch, as every good fishing cabin should have. For over a century this great lodge has catered to anglers searching for the finest in remote north woods fishing for landlocked salmon, trout, smallmouth bass, and lake trout.

From the rustic cabins, to the venerable main lodge, to the simple but extraordinarily satisfying Maine fare, Weatherby's offers a window into the history and tradition of great New England sport fishing.

SMOKED SAUSAGE AND BEAN SOUP

2   tablespoons butter
2   slices bacon, diced
1   garlic clove, minced
1   medium onion, diced
1/2 green pepper, diced
1   pound smoked sausage, cut into bite-size pieces
2   cups baked beans (homemade preferred)
1   quart half-and-half

Melt the butter in a skillet over medium-high heat. Sauté the bacon, garlic, onion, and green pepper until the bacon is crisp. In a soup pot combine the sautéed mixture with the sausage and baked beans and simmer at least 10 minutes. Add the half-and-half and heat through.

Makes 6 servings.

APPLES SAUTÉED WITH THYME

3   McIntosh or Cortland apples, cored
2   tablespoons butter
1   teaspoon fresh thyme leaves
1   teaspoon grated lemon zest
     Coarse salt
     Ground pepper

Cut each apple into 8 wedges and halve the wedges crosswise. Heat the butter in a large skillet over medium heat. Add the apples, thyme, and lemon zest. Season with salt and pepper to taste. Cook, tossing occasionally, until the apples are just tender when pierced with the tip of a knife, approximately 3 to 5 minutes.

Makes 4 servings.

ROASTED PORK WITH A FRUIT WINE SAUCE

1   cup assorted dried fruits (such as apricots, cherries, apples, cranberries)
1   cup dry red wine
1   boneless center-cut pork loin roast (about 4 pounds)
1   tablespoon olive oil
2   teaspoons chopped fresh thyme leaves (or 1 teaspoon dried)
1 1/2 teaspoons coarse salt
1/2 teaspoon freshly ground pepper
1/2 cup water
1 1/2 cups crumbled blue cheese

Preheat the oven to 500°. In a small bowl, soak the dried fruits in the red wine and set aside.

Rub the pork roast with the olive oil, then season with the thyme, salt, and pepper. Place the roast in a shallow roasting pan. Pour the water into the pan, place in oven, and roast for 30 minutes. Reduce the heat to 325° and continue roasting for 45 minutes to 1 hour, or until the temperature in the thickest part of the roast reads 150°. Transfer to serving platter and keep warm.

Remove any excess fat from the roasting pan. Drain the dried fruit, reserving wine. Add the reserved wine to the roasting pan and boil gently on the stovetop, removing any browned bits from the bottom of the pan. Reduce the sauce by half. Add the dried fruit to the pan and heat through.

Cut the meat into thin slices. Spoon the sauce over the meat and top with the crumbled blue cheese.

Makes 4 to 6 servings.

RASPBERRY PIE

Crust

2	cups all-purpose flour
	Dash salt
	Dash cinnamon
3/4	cup shortening
6	tablespoons ice water

Filling

4	cups raspberries
1 1/2	cups sugar
1/4	cup dry tapioca
1	tablespoon lemon juice

For the crust, in a bowl mix the flour, salt, and cinnamon. Cut in the shortening with a pastry blender or fork. Add about 6 tablespoons ice water (just until dough sticks together) and mix. Roll out onto a floured surface, making two 10-inch rounds. Place one of the dough rounds into a pie plate, pressing it into the bottom and side of the plate and trimming of the excess dough.

For the filling, preheat the oven to 425°. Mix the raspberries, sugar, tapioca, and lemon juice together in a bowl and pour into the piecrust. Seal with top crust and pierce with a fork to allow the steam to escape. Bake for approximately 1 hour, until the crust is golden and the filling is hot and bubbly.

Makes 8 servings.

Northwest
WHERE MIGHTY RIVERS FLOW

Flying B Ranch
Minette Bay Lodge
Morrison's Rogue River Lodge
Three Rivers Ranch
Wapiti Meadow Ranch

FLYING B RANCH

Kamiah, Idaho

Lewis and Clark were the first white men to see this part of the country, and in many ways it has not changed since they moved through here some 200 years ago. Places remain where you can look out across an unspoiled vista that is much the same as it was when the Corps of Discovery pushed through the American West. Central Idaho is rugged and spectacular, and it is here that one of the most diverse hunting and fishing adventures in the country is offered by the Flying B Ranch.

Flying B Ranch is a hunting and fishing lodge near the town of Kamiah (Kam-e-i) in central Idaho. Whether high in the alpine lakes, or deep in the Nez Perce National Forest, there are over 740,000 acres of the most extraordinary and dramatic country North America has to offer.

Perhaps the most remarkable thing about Flying B is the sheer diversity of what an outdoorsman can pursue in this great wilderness. Unlike most lodges, Flying B offers both hunting and fishing opportunities. Depending on the time of year and the season, trout, salmon, steelhead, deer, turkey, bear, elk, cougar, and a wide variety of upland bird species are available to the hunting and fishing patron. Chukar, quail, huns, and pheasant are plentiful and if nothing else, watching the dogs of Flying B work is a joy to devoted upland

hunters. Even in January, the coldest month of the year, booking a bird hunt is guaranteed to be a great experience since the snow cover is minimal and the temperature moderate.

The 14,000-square-foot log lodge is built in traditional western style and offers fourteen

guest rooms and can house twenty guests at one time. A sauna, Jacuzzi, and other amenities are available to soothe the tired hunter. However, the grand finale of the day is the bountiful table.

A number of Flying B's best game recipes use species native to the property. The recipes on the following pages are offered from the lodge kitchen and are reminiscent of country that still stirs the soul some 200 years after its discovery.

WILTED SPINACH SALAD WITH WARM BACON VINAIGRETTE

Red Wine Vinaigrette

1/3 cup red wine vinegar

1/2 medium onion, finely diced

1 tablespoon fresh thyme (or 1 1/2 teaspoons dried)

2 tablespoons sugar

1/2 teaspoon salt

1/2 teaspoon freshly ground pepper

1 cup light extra-virgin olive oil

Wilted Spinach Salad

6 to 8 pieces bacon, chopped and cooked, drippings reserved

1/2 cup brandy

1/3 cup Cointreau (Grand Marnier may be substituted)

Juice of 1 lemon

1/4 cup Dijon mustard

2/3 cup red wine vinaigrette (see previous recipe)

1 pound washed stemmed spinach

1 cup shredded Parmesan cheese

1/2 teaspoon freshly ground pepper

Parmesan cheese for garnish

For the vinaigrette, whisk together the vinegar, onion, thyme, sugar, salt, and pepper. Gradually whisk in the oil.

For the salad, in a medium saucepan heat the bacon in a few tablespoons of the reserved drippings. Pour the brandy and Cointreau over the bacon and ignite. Be careful of the flames. Once the flames have subsided add the lemon juice and mustard. Add 2/3 cup of the red wine vinaigrette. Sauté until the vinaigrette is slowly boiling. Place the spinach in a large mixing bowl and drizzle the hot vinaigrette over it. Sprinkle the Parmesan over the spinach and place a pan over the bowl and allow the spinach to steam for 1 minute. Remove the pan and toss to fully coat the spinach with the dressing. Serve immediately with pepper and garnish with Parmesan cheese.

Makes 6 servings.

MAPLE GLAZED BACON-WRAPPED CHUKAR

This recipe is very easy, but loved by everyone.

12 Chukar breasts (pheasant maybe substituted, but use 6 to 8 breasts)

12 slices thick cut smoked bacon

1/2 cup pure maple syrup

Preheat the oven to 400°. Cut each Chukar or pheasant in half lengthwise, making 24 pieces. Cut the bacon slices in half and wrap a piece of bacon around each piece of Chukar. It may be necessary to fold the Chukar in half so that it fits into the bacon when wrapped up. Place the Chukar on a greased baking sheet or use parchment paper to line a baking sheet. Place in the oven and bake until the bacon is mostly crisp. Remove from oven and brush each piece with maple syrup. Place back in oven and bake until nicely crisp (remove before the syrup begins to burn). Brush once more with syrup and let cool slightly. Serve on a platter with frill toothpicks.

Makes 6 servings.

HUCKLEBERRY SOUFFLÉ WITH HUCKLEBERRY SAUCE

Pastry Cream
5   large egg yolks (reserve the egg whites for the soufflé recipe below)

2/3 cup sugar

1/4 cup all-purpose flour

2   tablespoons cornstarch

1 1/2 cups 2% milk

Huckleberry Sauce
2   to 3 cups huckleberries (raspberries may be substituted)

1   6-ounce can pineapple juice

3/4 cup sugar

1   tablespoon vanilla extract

2   tablespoons cornstarch, combined with enough water to make a thin paste

1/2 pastry cream (see recipe above)

Soufflé
12   egg whites (make sure there is no residual egg yolk present)

1   teaspoon cream of tartar

1   pint heavy whipping cream

1/4 cup sugar

For the pastry cream, place the yolks in a mixing bowl and whisk in the sugar. Next, whisk in the flour and cornstarch until fully combined. Meanwhile place the milk in a double boiler over medium heat and scald. Slowly add the scalded milk to the egg yolk mixture and whisk until combined. Pour the contents back into the double boiler and place back on the burner over medium to medium-low heat. Cook, while continuously whisking, until the mixture has become very thick. Remove from the heat and set off to the side to cool. Remember to whisk occasionally so that the pastry cream doesn't form a skin.

For the sauce, in a medium saucepan bring the huckleberries and pineapple juice to a boil over medium heat. Add the sugar and vanilla and stir to combine. Add the cornstarch mixture while stirring and reduce the heat to medium-low. Once the sauce has thickened, remove from the heat and cool. Place half of the pastry cream in a mixing bowl with half of the huckleberry sauce. Mix thoroughly.

For the soufflé, preheat the oven to 350°. Butter and sugar eight 8-ounce soufflé cups. Place a 13x9-inch baking pan with 1 inch of water in the oven. Place the egg whites in a mixer and beat with the cream of tartar until stiff peaks form. Fold the whites into the remaining pastry cream, being careful not to over mix. Spoon the batter into the prepared soufflé cups, and place the cups into the water bath in the oven. Bake until the soufflés are golden on top and have risen 2 to 3 inches, about 15 to 25 minutes.

While the soufflé is baking, beat the whipping cream with the sugar until stiff peaks form. Place the whipped cream into a small serving bowl, and pour the huckleberry sauce over the top. Serve the soufflé straight from the oven with the huckleberry cream.

Makes 8 servings.

MINETTE BAY LODGE
Kitimat, British Columbia, Canada

At the top of the Douglas Channel in British Columbia, one of the world's great fjords, is a magnificent paradox. One of the most civilized lodges is at the edge of one of the most beautiful and untouched wilderness areas. While the lodge is reasonably easy to access as it lies on the outskirts of a thriving Haida village, it is at the gateway to some of the most spectacular glacial wilderness in the Canadian Northwest.

While one would expect a rugged and rustic log lodge in a place where eagles soar, grizzlies roam, and salmon come to spawn, at Minette Bay is a most civilized and tasteful lodge, not in a modern sense, but a classic, simple Victorian. It's almost as if a wealthy industrialist decided to move to the great northwest and brought his wife. The resulting house, while simple and tasteful in a most appealing and almost eastern maritime architecture, spares no opportunity to offer its visitors great comfort and pleasure in its down-comforter amenities. Comfort here is a priority.

Myriad adventures await visitors at the lodge, from fishing remarkable steelhead and salmon runs, to viewing grizzlies feeding in their native wilderness. Kayaking in an estuarine fjord and hiking in alpine meadows on the edge of glaciers are easily accessible and very close because Minette Bay Lodge uses a fleet of helicopters to place its guests where they want to be and doing what they want to do.

The Douglas Channel is a spectacular ecosystem. Within it is the Kitlope estuary and the largest untouched coastal watershed in the world with more than one million acres of pristine and untouched wilderness with thousand-year-old spruce and cedar trees. Minette Bay guests can go into the wilderness by jet boat and then be left alone to kayak to a remote camp for an evening of great food, big fires, and the stories of the Haida people told by the elders, and then a comfortable night in private wall tents.

The fishing season runs through the summer, and anglers are treated to some of the best salmon, steelhead, and trout fishing in the world, from glacier to estuary, all accessible by helicopter. Each day they are taken from great fishing hole to great fishing hole by their pilot guides.

Minette Bay Lodge is unique. The seventy-five-acre estate at the edge of Kitimat village is an oasis of old-world European comfort in a wilderness that is unchanged since the dawn of man. Surrounded by the Haida culture of totems and great cedar canoes, primeval temperate rainforests, and glacial mountain rivers, Minette Bay Lodge is a remarkable destination for those who want to immerse themselves in the wilderness during the day and surround themselves in simple but elegant comfort at night. It is an old world experience in an ancient environment—is a rare and wonderful combination.

TANGO SOUP

- 2 large (1/2 pound each) boiled potatoes, peeled and coarsely chopped
- 2 medium onions, coarsely chopped
- 2 celery hearts (inner pale stalks with leaves), coarsely chopped
- 2 large Granny Smith apples, peeled and coarsely chopped
- 2 firm-ripe bananas, coarsely chopped
- 2 pints chicken broth
- 2 cups heavy cream
- 2 tablespoons unsalted butter
- 2 rounded teaspoons curry powder
- 2 teaspoons salt
- 2 tablespoons chopped fresh chives

In a heavy 3-quart saucepan simmer the potatoes, onions, celery hearts, apples, and bananas in the chicken broth, covered, until very tender (about 12 minutes). Stir in the cream, butter, curry powder, and salt. Heat just until hot; do not boil.

Purée the soup in batches in a blender until smooth. Do not fill the blender more than three-quarters full and be sure to cover it with a towel when blending to prevent burning. Return the puréed soup to the saucepan. Thin the soup with water if desired. Serve sprinkled with chives.

Note: Use caution when blending hot liquids.

Makes 8 to 12 servings.

FLAMING PRAWNS

- 1 tablespoon olive oil
- 1 teaspoon minced garlic
- 24 large prawns, peeled and deveined
- 1/2 cup roasted sweet red peppers, coarsely chopped
- 1/2 cup canned Italian plum tomatoes, well-drained and coarsely chopped
- 1/2 cup crumbled feta cheese
- 1/4 cup fresh basil leaves
- 1/2 seeded lemon
- 1 ounce ouzo (in a shot glass or small glass)

In a large frying pan heat the olive oil over high heat. Add the garlic and when it sizzles add the prawns. Stir-fry until the prawns turn pink. Add the roasted peppers and tomatoes and stir-fry until the prawns are cooked through.

While the prawns are cooking, heat a heavy (preferably cast iron) frying pan over high heat. Set a wooden board next to the stove on which to place the hot frying pan. Place the lemon and ouzo at the place where you are going to flame the prawns.

Add the feta and basil to the prawns and stir to combine. Spoon the mixture into the hot frying pan, pushing it to one side of the pan. Place the pan on the wooden board. Carry the board to the presentation area and advise everyone to stay back. Squeeze the lemon over the prawns. Add ouzo and then ignite.

Makes 4 appetizer-size servings.

MAPLE WHISKEY GLAZED SALMON

Maple syrup, whiskey, and salmon give this rich recipe a taste of Canada. Serve it with small new potatoes and seasonal vegetables.

4   6-ounce salmon fillets or steaks
    Salt and freshly cracked black pepper to taste
3   tablespoons maple syrup
2   tablespoons whiskey
1   tablespoon Dijon mustard
    Juice from 1/2 lemon
2   teaspoons chopped fresh dill
    Dill sprigs and lemon wedges for garnish

Preheat the oven 425°F. Place the salmon in a shallow baking dish. Season with salt and pepper. Combine the maple syrup, whiskey, mustard, lemon juice, and chopped dill in a bowl. Mix well and spoon over the fish. Bake for 12 to 15 minutes, or until the fish begins to flake slightly.

Divide the salmon among 4 plates and spoon the pan juices over. Garnish with dill sprigs and lemon wedges.

Makes 4 servings.

ALDER-SMOKED SOCKEYE SALMON SALAD WITH FIRE-GRILLED TOMATO VINAIGRETTE AND BALSAMIC SYRUP

1/2 cup plus 2 teaspoons balsamic vinegar

2   medium tomatoes

3/4 teaspoon plus 1/4 cup olive oil

1   shallot, finely diced

1   garlic clove, minced

3   tablespoons canola oil

3   tablespoons red wine vinegar

1/2 teaspoon freshly ground black pepper
    Salt to taste

5   ounces fresh goat cheese

4   4-ounce pieces sockeye salmon

4   cups mesclun greens

4   chives

Place 1/2 cup of the balsamic vinegar in a small saucepan over medium heat and bring to a boil. Reduce the heat and simmer for about 5 minutes or until it is reduced to 3 tablespoons. Remove from the heat and set aside to cool.

Preheat the grill to low. Soak a handful of alder chips in water for 10 minutes.

Cut the tomatoes in half crosswise. Squeeze the tomatoes and discard the seeds. Place the tomatoes in a small mixing bowl. Add 3/4 teaspoon of the olive oil and toss. Place the tomatoes on the grill for 3 minutes per side. Remove and cool.

While the tomatoes are cooling, whisk together the shallot, garlic, the remaining 1/4 cup olive oil, the canola oil, red wine vinegar, the remaining 2 teaspoons balsamic vinegar, pepper, and salt to taste in a small bowl. Dice the grilled tomatoes and add to the vinaigrette. Stir just to coat.

Using two teaspoons, form 1/2 ounce of soft goat cheese into an oval (quenelle). Repeat, making 3 quenelles per plate (12 quenelles total). You could also crumble the cheese over the finished salad.

Increase the heat of the grill to medium. Grill the salmon for about 3 minutes per side or until firm to the touch. Divide the mesclun greens among 4 plates and place the grilled salmon on top. Drizzle the tomato vinaigrette over the salmon and greens. Place the quenelles at three points around each salad. Drizzle the balsamic syrup around the perimeter. Cut the chives in half and place criss-crossed over the salmon. Serve immediately.

Makes 4 servings.

MORRISON'S
ROGUE RIVER LODGE

Merlin, Oregon

When thinking of the great Northwest, one envisions dark coniferous forests clinging to the flanks of great mountain ranges, cut by rowdy rivers that rush and plunge their way to the Pacific. Perhaps the most notable of these and the most aptly named is the Rogue River. Named after the Takelma Indians who, because of their dogged defense of their homeland, were named les Coquins or rogues by the early French Canadian trappers, the Rogue River rises in the volcanic Cascade Range and drops to the Pacific through the Siskiyou Mountains. The 1.8 million acres of the Rogue River-Siskiyou National Forest are in a temperate rainforest so botanically diverse as to be rivaled only by the Eastern Smoky Mountains.

Spanning the border of Northern California and Southern Oregon, this magnificent wilderness offers some of the best fishing in the world, and the Rogue River is particularly noted for its Steelhead run, the big ocean-run rainbows that migrate to the ocean and return to the rivers of their birth in the fall. These are spectacular fighting game fish that grow much larger and stronger than their fresh water cousins and as such have a following of anglers that is almost cultish.

In the 1920s Zane Gray spent time on the Rogue in pursuit of his favored "half-pounders," immature Steelhead that return to the river early and are well known for their tenacious fighting ability. These fish are found only in three rivers: the Rogue, the Klamath, and the Eel. It was the Rogue that set the scene for his book *Rogue River Feud* published in 1929.

On the banks of the Rogue near Grant's Pass is Morrison's Rogue River Lodge. The lodge was built in 1945 by Lloyd Morrison, a lumberman and fishing guide who, with the financial help of a few clients, built the lodge using handpicked bird's-eye pine which over the years has developed a rich, dark patina giving the lodge a well-deserved look of permanence and tradition—a look that is highly prized in great sporting lodges that have stood the test of time.

Today the lodge is run by Michelle Hanten whose family has run the lodge for the past thirty-three years. In addition to spectacular fishing, there is white water rafting on the Rogue, which was designated a Wild and Scenic River in the 1970s and was the set for Meryl Streep's *The River Wild*. Morrison's was one of the original lodges to create whitewater rafting trips in the United States. The original lodge is the centerpiece of the grounds surrounded by nine separate river-view cabins.

The dining is superb and Morrison's reputation for fine cuisine has been notably highlighted twice by *Bon Appétit* magazine for its Oregon Griddle Cakes and Apple Walnut Torte with Caramel Sauce.

There are few places in the world that offer the grandeur of the great American Northwest. It is a place where rivers are perhaps more spectacular in their wanderings through cliffs and canyons, where vast expanses of wilderness still exist covered in dark green forests, where the floor of the forest is open and the canopy of evergreens dense and cool. For more than seventy years, Morrison's Rogue River Lodge has resided in these environs as a haven of grace and hospitality in a rough-and-tumble country.

HERB ENCRUSTED TENDERLOIN OF BEEF

1   cup pomegranate juice concentrate
1   cup Syrah Port
1/2 cup demi-glace (made with 1/2 cup of boiling water and 2 tablespoons glace de viande)
8   8-ounce beef tenderloin steaks
1/4 cup extra-virgin olive oil
     Salt and pepper to taste
     Equal parts of chopped fresh rosemary, thyme, oregano, chives, and parsley

Combine the pomegranate concentrate and Syrah Port in a saucepan over medium-high heat and cook until reduced by half.

Add the demi-glace and incorporate until well blended and smooth. Set the sauce aside.

Preheat the oven to 500°. Brush the steaks with olive oil, season with salt and pepper, and coat with the herb mixture. In an ovenproof pan heat the olive oil over high heat. Sear the steaks in the pan for 1 minute on each side.

Place the pan in the oven and cook to the desired degree of doneness, about 4 minutes for medium-rare.

Place the steaks on a serving plate and ladle the sauce on top of the steaks. Serve with baked potatoes and cream and roasted baby root vegetables.

Makes 8 servings.

POACHED PEARS WITH SUGARED AFRICAN VIOLETS

2   cups Pinot Noir or Gamay Beaujolais
1   cup sugar
2   cups cranberry juice
1   cinnamon stick
6   allspice berries
4   whole cloves
8   Bosc pears, blemish-free with stems attached
     African violet flowers
     Sugar

Combine the wine, sugar, cranberry juice, cinnamon stick, allspice berries, and cloves in a saucepan and bring to a boil. Peel the pears, leaving the stems attached. Reduce the heat to medium-low and poach the pears in the wine until just tender, at least 20 minutes. Remove from the heat and leave the pears in the poaching liquid until they take on a rose color. Remove the pears and set aside.

Strain the poaching liquid, reserving the liquid in the saucepan and discarding the spices. Cook the sauce over low heat until it becomes reduced to heavy syrup.

Brush African violet flowers with the syrup and dip in sugar. This will harden the flowers a bit.

Puddle the syrup onto a dessert plate and place the poached pears in the syrup. Place a flower crystal on each pear at the base of the stem.

Makes 8 servings.

SCARLET AUTUMN SALAD

Blackberry Vinaigrette

1/2 cup red wine vinegar

1/2 cup blackberry juice (from frozen or fresh berries)

3 garlic cloves, pressed or minced

1 teaspoon salt

1 teaspoon medium-grind black pepper

1/4 cup sugar

1 to 1 1/2 cups canola oil

Note: If using fresh berries process in a food processor, strain the juice, and discard the seeds.

Salad

10 ounces red mesclun salad mix (mixture of baby red leaf, red oak leaf, radicchio, and/or red baby romaine)

12 ounces goat cheese coated in herbes de Provence

1 cup pickled shoestring beets, drained

1 cup pickled red onion, drained

Black cherry rose petals for garnish

For the vinaigrette, in a medium bowl, combine the vinegar, blackberry juice, garlic, salt, pepper, and sugar. Slowly whisk in the canola oil.

For the salad, toss the greens with half of the vinaigrette. Place the salad mixture in the center of each plate and top with a slice of goat cheese. Place the beets and onions around the salad and add additional vinaigrette if needed. Garnish with black cherry rose petals around the edge of the salad.

Makes 8 servings.

THREE RIVERS RANCH
Warm River, Idaho

When anglers talk of fishing in the west, Colorado and Montana are most frequently mentioned, and then, of course, Yellowstone in Wyoming. But the great unsung bastion of spectacular fishing is in Idaho. It is a remarkable state with more wilderness area than any other state in the lower forty-eight, and some of the hallowed cathedrals of fly fishing are here—Henry's Fork for example.

While most tourists flock to the front side of the Tetons, it is the back side where anglers who truly know the west find some of the best fishing not only in the west, but perhaps in the world. It is here, dead center behind the Teton Range, that Three Rivers Ranch sits on Robinson Creek.

Three Rivers is old—old as in venerable, experienced, calm, comfortable, and confident. Lonnie Allen has been doing this for a lot of years and her head guide, Doug Gibson, is an example of the quiet strength and incredible knowledge of the veteran western fishing guide. There is nothing fancy here—extremely comfortable, yes; fancy, no. There are amenities here for anglers, but no frills: comfortable cabins with rod racks outside, a beautiful old lodge with a magnificent mahogany bar, and a beautiful setting along the creek. In a word, this is the kind of camp that anglers dream about, where great fishing is first and foremost and set in the midst of some of the most beautiful landscapes imaginable.

Three Rivers is uniquely positioned at the heart of the West's most enjoyable and challenging fly fishing, with the Fall River, Teton River, Warm River, and the legendary Henry's Fork within a short walk or drive from the guest cabins. With the immense Grand Tetons towering in the distance as you drive to the river, framed by big skies and great stands of lodgepole pines, it's no wonder many return year after year.

There are also opportunities to float the south fork of the Snake or the Yellowstone, wade the Gibbon, fish the legendary Railroad Ranch on the Henry's Fork or the Gallatin and the Firehole. You can float the Madison or, even better, spend the night at the outpost camp on the South Fork where there are 7,000 fish per mile and one of the best cutthroat fisheries anywhere.

Lonnie and Doug have been doing this for twenty-five years. They know two things: how to make you feel welcome and comfortable, and how to custom tailor your fishing adventure exactly as you want it and then provide that experience with the expertise that only years on these rivers can provide. There are not two nicer people in this business.

Are there fancier lodges in the west? Probably. Are there any that know their job as well as Three Rivers? No. One trip here and it's pretty certain you will return. It's that good.

COLESLAW

1   cup vinegar
1 1/2 cups sugar
2/3   cup oil
1   teaspoon salt
1   small onion, finely chopped
2   carrots, shredded
1   medium head cabbage, shredded
1   red bell pepper, chopped

In a saucepan combine the vinegar, sugar, oil, and salt and bring to a boil. Cool in the refrigerator. The mixture will be slightly thick.

Combine the onion, carrots, cabbage, and red pepper in a large bowl. Pour the dressing over the coleslaw and toss to coat.

Note: Keeps very well for one week.

Makes 6 to 8 servings.

COCKTAIL MEATBALLS

1   pound ground beef
1/2   cup dry bread crumbs
1/3   cup finely chopped onion
1/4   cup milk
1   tablespoon chopped fresh parsley
1   teaspoon salt
1   teaspoon Worcestershire sauce
1/8   teaspoon pepper
1   egg
1/4   cup shortening
1   12-ounce bottle chili sauce
1   10-ounce jar grape jelly

In a large bowl, mix the ground beef, bread crumbs, onion, milk, parsley, salt, Worcestershire sauce, pepper, and egg. Shape into 1-inch balls.

In a 12-inch skillet melt the shortening. Cook the meatballs in the shortening until brown. Remove the meatballs from the skillet and drain the fat. Heat the chili sauce and jelly in the skillet, stirring constantly until the jelly is melted. Add the meatballs and stir until coated. Simmer, uncovered, for 30 minutes. Serve hot.

Makes 5 dozen meatballs.

DILLY OF A MUSHROOM SOUP

2   tablespoons butter, divided
2 1/2 cups chopped onions
1   pound sliced mushrooms
2   teaspoons dried dill weed
2 1/2 teaspoons paprika
4   teaspoons soy sauce
2 1/2 cups chicken stock, divided
2   tablespoons all-purpose flour
1 3/4 cups skim milk
3/4 cup sour cream or nonfat yogurt
2 1/2 teaspoons lemon juice
     Sour cream or nonfat yogurt for garnish
     Croutons for garnish

In a large saucepan melt 1 tablespoon of the butter. Add the onions and cook until tender. Add the mushrooms, dill, paprika, soy sauce, and 3/4 cup of the stock. Bring to a boil, reduce the heat, and simmer for 15 minutes.

In a small saucepan, melt the remaining tablespoon butter and add the flour. Whisk for 1 minute. Gradually add the milk. Whisk continuously until the mixture thickens. Add several ladles of the soup to the milk mixture and whisk together. Pour the milk mixture into soup mixture and add the remaining 1 3/4 cups stock. Cover and simmer for 15 minutes.

To serve, ladle the soup in serving bowls and top each with 1 teaspoon of sour cream or nonfat yogurt and 3 or 4 croutons.

Makes 6 to 8 servings.

PANNA COTTA

Panna Cotta
3   tablespoons water
1   tablespoon unflavored gelatin
3   cups heavy cream
1/2 cup milk
1/2 cup buttermilk
1/3 cup sugar
     Pinch salt
1   teaspoon pure vanilla extract

Mango Sauce
2   cups orange juice (not concentrate)
1/2 cup sugar
2   fresh mangos, diced

For the panna cotta, pour the water into a small bowl and sprinkle the gelatin over it. Set aside until the gelatin is softened, about 5 minutes.

Mix together the cream, milk, buttermilk, sugar, and salt in a large heavy saucepan. Bring to a boil, stirring frequently. Remove from the heat and add the gelatin mixture. Stir until the gelatin is melted.

Transfer the mixture to a large bowl set inside a larger bowl of ice water. Stir gently with a rubber spatula until the mixture is cool to the touch and slightly thicker than heavy cream. Pour the mixture into twelve 4-ounce ramekins. Refrigerate for at least 3 hours.

For the sauce, place the orange juice and sugar in a medium saucepan and boil down until thick. Cool completely. Add the fresh mangos to the cooked mixture.

To serve, unmold the panna cotta onto serving plates. Spoon the mango sauce over the panna cotta, letting it run over the edge.

Note: To unmold the ramekins place them in very warm tap water for about 30 seconds, and then slide a knife around the edges of the panna cotta and invert the ramekins onto a serving plate.

Makes 12 servings.

WAPITI MEADOW RANCH
Cascade, Idaho

Wapiti is Shawnee for "elk," of which there is no shortage here, along with moose, wolves, mountain lions, bears, and herds of mule deer. This ultra-remote fishing lodge is on the edge of the Frank Church River of No Return Wilderness, the largest and most remote area still left in the lower forty-eight states. A road map of Idaho shows a huge blank area where roads and access simply do not exist. It carries many names, the Empty Quarter, the Margins, the Yonlands, America's Outback, but no matter what name it is given, this area is virtually unchanged since the first white man viewed it, which unfortunately cannot be said for most lands upon which the white man has trod.

In this last great wilderness lies Wapiti Meadow Ranch, a remarkable blend of rugged mountain lodge and comfortable amenities reflecting the personality of founders and owners Diana and Barry Bryant. Diana, a Virginia aristocrat raised in the horse country of the east, married Barry, whose family has been on this land for four generations and knows this country intimately. Together they have opened a window to this wilderness with amenities and comforts never imagined in these mountains.

At the heart of the ranch is a massive stone and log structure with an eclectic mix of western charm and Virginia graciousness that reflects the personalities of the two owners. Sitting on the front porch, one looks at a view that is unchanged and still unspoiled since the first white man reached this country. That alone is worth the visit. That one can fish for trout and salmon in untouched wild streams and alpine lakes still devoid of man's meddling nature, ride horses into the wilderness and never see another human, or sit in a hot tub and listen to wolves howl in the night, is all the more reason to come here.

Prior to creating Wapiti with Barry, Diana owned a gourmet catering business in Washington, D.C. She brings to this wilderness a rare and professional approach to food and gracious entertaining that seems incongruent in a place so removed from civilization. Yet here in her lodge is an island of cordial hospitality in the heart of an untamed and unsettled land. The Wapiti Meadow Ranch can satisfy the desires of those travelers who wish to see this country as Lewis and Clark saw it, but want to enjoy comforts and excellent cuisine based on native food sources such as salmon, duck, and elk.

SENEGALESE SOUP

3	Granny Smith apples
2	tablespoons butter
2	carrots, chopped
1	large white onion, chopped
1/4	cup raisins
1	garlic clove, chopped
3	tablespoons curry powder
2	tablespoons flour
8	cups chicken broth
1	tablespoon canned tomato purée
1/2	cup heavy cream
	Salt to taste
	Prepared mango chutney if desired

Peel, core, and chop the apples. In a heavy kettle heat the butter over moderate heat until the foam subsides. Add the apples, carrots, onion, raisins, and garlic, stirring occasionally, cooking until they begin to soften, approximately 10 to 12 minutes. Add the curry powder and cook, stirring for 1 minute. Add the flour and cook, stirring for 2 minutes. Stir in the broth and tomato purée and simmer, covered, for 1 hour and 20 minutes. Stir in the cream and salt to taste and simmer, uncovered, for 10 minutes.

Cool the soup. Purée in a food processor or blender in batches until smooth. If necessary, strain the soup through a sieve into a large bowl and chill until cold, approximately 2 to 3 hours.

Garnish each serving with 1/2 teaspoon chutney if desired.

Note: The soup is best if made a day ahead of serving.

Makes 10 servings.

MUSTARD SEED ENCRUSTED SALMON

1/2	cup dry white wine
1/4	cup chopped shallots
3	tablespoons yellow mustard seeds, divided
3/4	cup whipping cream
5	tablespoons whole grain Dijon mustard, divided
1	tablespoon chopped fresh tarragon
	Salt and pepper to taste
1	8-ounce salmon fillet
2	tablespoons butter

Boil the wine, shallots and 1 tablespoon of the mustard seeds in a heavy small saucepan until the mixture is reduced to 1/2 cup, approximately 2 minutes. Whisk in the cream, 2 1/2 tablespoons of the Dijon mustard, and the tarragon. Boil until thickened to sauce consistency, approximately 3 minutes. Season with salt and pepper. Remove from heat and cover.

Preheat the oven to 350°. Brush the salmon on both sides with remaining 2 1/2 tablespoons Dijon mustard. Sprinkle remaining 2 tablespoons mustard seeds, and salt and pepper onto both sides of the salmon. Wrap tightly in aluminum foil and bake for 30 minutes to 1 hour, depending upon the size of the fillet.

Transfer to a platter after baking and spoon the mustard sauce over the fillet.

Makes 4 servings.

SPINACH AND GORGONZOLA CASSEROLE

Butter for coating
1   10-ounce package frozen chopped spinach, thawed and undrained
1   16-ounce container small-curd cottage
4   ounces (1 cup) crumbled Gorgonzola cheese
1/4 cup melted butter
3   tablespoons flour
    Salt and pepper to taste
5   large beaten eggs

Preheat the oven to 350°. Lightly coat an 11x7-inch baking dish with butter. Place the spinach in a large bowl. Mix in the cottage cheese, Gorgonzola cheese, melted butter, and flour. Season to taste with salt and pepper. Add the eggs and stir until well blended. Transfer the mixture to the prepared dish.

Bake until set in the center, about 1 hour and 15 minutes. Let stand 10 minutes before serving.

Makes 6 side-dish servings.

GRILLED TOMATO HALVES

4   tomatoes
4   tablespoons olive oil
2   garlic cloves, crushed
1   tablespoon chopped fresh basil
    Shredded Parmesan

Slice the tomatoes in half (or if small, slice the top quarter off). Remove a thin slice from bottom if necessary to make the tomato stand. Place the tomato halves on a jelly-roll pan lined with foil or in low-sided casserole dish.

Combine the oil, garlic, and basil in a small bowl. Spread the mixture on each cut half. Sprinkle generously with Parmesan. Allow to stand at least 1 hour. Just before serving, put under the broiler until the cheese is golden and the tomatoes are warm.

Makes 4 to 8 side-dish servings.

Rockies
CATHEDRAL OF THE TROUT

CANYON RANCH

Big Horn, Wyoming

If one can tell the quality of someone by the caliber of his friends, perhaps one can tell the quality of a lodge by the caliber of the guests. Queen Elizabeth and Prince Phillip, French President Valery Giscard d'Estaing and other notables have all been guests at Canyon Ranch.

Oliver Wallop, who founded the ranch in 1888, was the eighth Earl of Portsmouth, a member of the Wyoming senate, and a legendary figure in Wyoming history. He was renowned for his horse breeding and, with his brother-in-law, was responsible for shipping thousands of horses to the British and American armies for the Boer and Spanish-American wars. The movie *Broken Trail* with Robert Duvall is loosely taken from this epic tale of Western enterprise.

Today Canyon Ranch, backed up to Wyoming's Big Horn Mountains, is as beautiful as ever and run by Paul and Sandra Wallop, the fourth generation of this remarkable family. Paul brings a wonderfully different and perhaps better perspective on fishing than most.

I personally do not much enjoy fishing popular waters, which often have many other fishermen competing for prime locations. Instead I prefer to fish for wild fish in wild places. I have fond memories of large trout I have caught in well known waters of the west, but the experiences I relish and stories I tell most often come from days catching fish in remote waters where beautiful surroundings and the day's adventures make the trip memorable. I enjoy the thrill of catching any fish that is a "trophy" in relative terms, to the waters of the day. I am always excited by the chance that the one fish, which has beaten the average and outgrown the general population, will rise from the depths of a picturesque "hole" and take my fly.

While the main lodge is spectacular, Johnny's Cabin is the pinnacle of the wilderness experience. High in the hills at the back of the ranch, the cabin has no electricity, but is lit and warmed by wood stoves and propane lights. Though it is rustic, one still sleeps under down comforters and high-count sheets. There is no one to bother you, though, as Paul puts it, "We will come check on you from time to time." High above one of the legendary and storied ranches in western history, in one of the most beautiful places in the world, for the lover of solitude and wilderness there can be no better experience than Johnny's Cabin. It is easy to see why the notables of the world have beaten a path to the gates of Canyon Ranch.

PERFECT GRILLED CHICKEN

Prepared the night before, the grilled chicken is an easily packed picnic lunch.

- 3/4 cup unseasoned rice vinegar
- 1/4 cup low-sodium soy sauce
  Juice of 1 lemon
- 1 to 2 garlic cloves, pressed
- 1/4 cup chopped fresh parsley or cilantro (or a mixture if you like)
- 1 teaspoon crushed red pepper
- 3/4 cup olive oil
- 6 to 8 chicken thighs

Combine the vinegar, soy sauce, lemon juice, garlic, parsley, red pepper, and olive oil in a shallow dish. Add the chicken and marinate in the refrigerator for 1 hour.

Preheat a charcoal or gas grill to medium heat. Cook the chicken for 12 to 15 minutes skin side up. Turn over and cook for 8 to 12 minutes. Remove and allow to cool. Refrigerate overnight. Pack with some chips, fresh fruit, and a few cookies.

Makes 3 to 4 servings.

SUMMER SALMON ON THE GRILL

Butter Mixture
- 1/2 cup (1 stick) organic butter, softened
- 2 shallots, chopped
- 2 tablespoons chopped fresh cilantro
  Juice of 1/2 lemon
- 1/2 teaspoon cayenne pepper

Salmon
- 1 whole salmon fillet
- 1/2 cup butter mixture

For the butter, using a fork or your fingers in a bowl mix the butter, shallots, cilantro, lemon juice, and cayenne pepper together thoroughly.

For the salmon, preheat a grill.

Make a foil tray big enough to hold the salmon. Spray with nonstick cooking spray and place the salmon on the tray. Pat the butter mixture evenly onto the salmon so that it will coat the entire salmon as it melts. Place the tray on the grill and cook over indirect heat for 15 to 20 minutes depending on the size of fillet.

Makes 4 servings.

GREEN BEANS WITH FENNEL

- 2 pounds washed, trimmed green beans
- 2 tablespoons olive oil
- 1 cup chopped fresh fennel
  Salt and Pepper

In a 3-quart pot cook the beans in boiling water just until tender. Drain and rinse immediately with cold water. In a sauté pan add the oil and heat very hot. Add the fennel and the green beans stirring rapidly to mix well. Remove from the heat. Add salt and pepper to taste and serve.

Makes 8 servings.

SAGE RUBBED GRILLED PORK TENDERLOIN

Mango Salsa

2   mangos, chopped
1/2 red onion, chopped
1   shallot, chopped
1   jalapeño pepper, seeded and chopped
1/2 cup chopped fresh cilantro
    Juice of 2 limes
1/4 cup pineapple juice
1   teaspoon rice wine vinegar or cider vinegar
    Salt and pepper to taste

Pork Tenderloin

3   tablespoons kosher salt
1   garlic clove, minced
3 to 4 fresh sage leaves, chopped
2   1-pound pork tenderloins
    Freshly ground pepper
    Olive Oil

For the mango salsa, in a bowl combine the mangos, onion, shallot, jalapeño, cilantro, lime juice, pineapple juice, vinegar, and salt and pepper to taste. Set aside.

Note: To vary the heat of the peppers add a serrano chile pepper instead of a jalapeño.

For the pork tenderloin, using a mortar and pestle, grind the salt, garlic, and sage until thoroughly mixed. Rub the mixture over each tenderloin and place in a shallow dish. Sprinkle with pepper and drizzle with olive oil until evenly coated.

Preheat a grill and cook the tenderloins over indirect heat for 20 to 30 minutes, or until the tenderloins reach an internal temperature of 150° to 160°.

Serve the mango salsa with the pork tenderloin.

Makes 8 servings.

HOMESTYLE SOUR CREAM MASHED POTATOES

3   pounds white potatoes
3   tablespoons butter
1   cup sour cream
    Salt and pepper

Peel and cut the potatoes into chunks. Bring to a boil. Cover over low heat until soft. Drain and return to the pot. Add the butter, sour cream, salt, and pepper. Mash the potatoes until thoroughly mixed. Do not worry about lumps as that contributes to the old-fashioned homestyle texture.

Makes 6 to 8 servings.

TOMATO CASSEROLE

2   pounds roma tomatoes, quartered
1/2 pound green beans, blanched
1 to 2 jars artichoke hearts
1   cup shredded mozzarella cheese
1/2 cup chopped fresh basil
1/4 cup Italian dressing

In a large bowl combine the tomatoes, green beans, artichoke hearts, mozzarella cheese, and basil. Add the Italian dressing and toss to coat.

Makes 8 servings.

APPLE CRISP

6   large Granny Smith apples
2   tablespoons lemon juice
1   cup water
1   cup oats
1   cup firmly packed brown sugar
2 1/2 tablespoons butter, cut into small pieces
1   teaspoon cinnamon
    Whipped cream for serving

Core and cut the apples into slices. Mix the apple slices with the lemon juice in a large bowl. In a heavy saucepan bring the water to a boil and add the apples and cook for 20 minutes. Remove from the heat. Drain the apples and place in a large bowl. Let cool for about 15 minutes. Combine the oats, brown sugar, butter, and cinnamon in a bowl and mix well. Set aside.

Preheat the oven to 350°. In a coated 13x9-inch pan add the apples and sprinkle the top with the oats mixture. Bake for 30 to 35 minutes. Serve with whipped cream.

Makes 4 to 6 servings.

CRAIG FELLIN OUTFITTERS AND BIG HOLE LODGE
Wise River, Montana

A small and often overlooked section in the southwest corner of Montana, cut off from the rest of the country by the Bitterroot, Pioneer, and Anaconda Mountain ranges, is home to one of the most beautiful and tragic river valleys in the Rockies—the Big Hole River Valley. Home to isolated ranches and farms, the Big Hole River flows north from its origins in the Bitterroot Range, moving slowly through the rich bottom land, then occasionally plunging through canyons until it joins with the Jefferson after a circumnavigation of the lowlands around the Pioneer Mountains.

There is not much here except for isolated farms in a valley known as the land of 10,000 haystacks. However, one of this nation's great tragedies took place nearby, at the Big Hole Battlefield. Chief Joseph and the Nez Perce tribe held off John Gibbon's cavalry force, with the loss of many of their men, women, and children. They succeeded in escaping only to be caught in October of 1877 just 40 miles from the Canadian border and safety. It was one of the most poignant and heartbreaking stories of the Native American in a western history fraught with such heartbreak.

In 1983 Craig Fellin and his wife Peggy bought a small cabin at the confluence of the Wise River and the Big Hole. They opened with room for two anglers. The only access at the time was eight miles of unimproved dirt road. Since then the lodge has grown to accommodate twelve anglers. The main lodge was built from lodge pole pine and river rock on the property. It fits this remote and quiet land—unassuming, but wonderfully comfortable—and offers fishing in what many seasoned anglers regard as the finest river in Montana.

Perhaps what sets this lodge apart, aside from its quiet location and extraordinary fishery, is the quality of the guides. The master guides at Big Hole Lodge have more than 100 years of fly fishing experience and come from all over the world, but each year they loyally return to spend their summers with Craig and Peggy in the Big Hole Valley. Most of the employees have been with the operation for over ten years, which says something about the owners and the quality of the experience that visitors will receive. Chef Lanette Evener is one such employee and is an accomplished angler as well as an accomplished chef.

The lodge offers three miles of private access to the Beaverhead River on a working cattle ranch leased since 1986. There is also a lease on a spring creek nearby with three miles of private water. Other rivers that can be fished include the Bitterroot, Rock Creek, and the Ruby.

While there are most certainly lodges with more elaborate facilities, Big Hole Lodge seems to fit its environs perfectly, offering some of the finest fishing in Montana, in one of the quietest and most beautiful corners of the state, a corner that is less traveled, but once discovered will beckon the angler again and again.

GRILLED SALMON WITH APPLE, CELERY, AND CHIVE RÉMOULADE

Rémoulade

1/2 cup mayonnaise

1 tablespoon fresh lemon juice

2 teaspoons Dijon mustard

1 tablespoon drained and chopped capers

1/2 cup minced chives, divided

2 Granny Smith apples, peeled and julienned

2 celery stalks, cut into 1/4-inch-thick slices
Pinch of salt and pepper

Mustard Dill Sauce

1/2 teaspoon dry mustard

1/2 cup Dijon mustard

1 1/2 tablespoons sugar

1 tablespoon white wine vinegar

2 tablespoons minced fresh dill (or 1 tablespoon dried)

1 1/2 tablespoons canola oil

1 1/2 tablespoons extra-virgin olive oil

Salmon

4 8-ounce skinless salmon fillets

3 tablespoons olive oil

12 sprigs chives for garnish

4 radishes, thinly sliced for garnish

For the rémoulade, in a medium bowl mix the mayonnaise, lemon juice, mustard, capers and 1 tablespoon of the minced chives. Add the apples and mix right away to prevent discoloring. Add the celery and a pinch of salt and pepper; set aside.

For the sauce, in a medium bowl or blender add the dry mustard, Dijon, sugar, vinegar and dill and stir. Slowly whisk in the canola oil and olive oil until emulsified; set aside.

For the salmon, heat a grill to medium–high heat. Rub the salmon fillets with the olive oil and sprinkle with salt and pepper. Grill the salmon fillets for 3 to 4 minutes on each side until done. Transfer to a plate.

To serve, spread the remaining minced chives on one side of each salmon fillet. Place the salmon, chive side up, on top of a bed of Forbidden Rice (recipe follows) and place 1/2 cup of the apple rémoulade on top of the salmon. Place a dollop of the Mustard Dill Sauce on the side. Garnish with 3 chive sprigs and sliced radishes.

Makes 4 servings.

ROASTED GARLIC AND BRIE SOUP

2	whole garlic bulbs
	Salt
4	tablespoons olive oil, divided
1	medium onion, finely diced
2	celery stalks, finely diced
1	carrot, finely diced
1/4	cup all-purpose flour
6	cups chicken broth
1	teaspoon chopped fresh oregano or 1/2 teaspoon dried
1/2	teaspoon chopped fresh thyme or 1/4 teaspoon dried
7	ounces Brie, rind removed and cubed
	Croutons or sourdough bread

Preheat the oven to 375°. Break the garlic bulbs into individual cloves, but do not peel them. Spread the cloves on a baking sheet, sprinkle with salt and drizzle with 1 tablespoon of the olive oil. Bake, shaking the pan occasionally, for about 30 minutes or until tender. Let cool.

Heat the remaining 3 tablespoons olive oil in a soup pot over medium-high heat. Add the onion and sauté for 10 minutes. Add the celery and carrots and sauté for 10 more minutes. Gradually add the flour and stir for 3 minutes until the vegetables are coated. Gradually stir in the chicken broth and bring to a boil, stirring frequently. Reduce the heat to medium-low and simmer, stirring occasionally, until slightly thickened, about 15 minutes.

Once the roasted garlic has cooled, peel the cloves. Place in a food processor with 1 cup of the soup and purée. Return the purée to the soup pot. Add the oregano and thyme and bring the soup to a simmer. Add the Brie, one cube at a time, stirring until melted. Season with salt and pepper to taste. Serve the soup with a crouton in the center or crispy sourdough on the side.

Makes 6 servings.

FORBIDDEN RICE

Forbidden rice is available at gourmet specialty stores and is short-grained heirloom rice that is black when raw and dark purple when cooked. The name comes from the legend that the rice was reserved for emperors in ancient China because of its nutritional value and rarity. The rice is high in fiber and has a deep nutty taste.

3/4	cup forbidden rice
3	tablespoons butter
1	shallot, minced
1	tablespoon peeled and grated fresh ginger
1/2	minced carrot
1	teaspoon crushed fennel seeds
1/2	cup white wine
1 1/4	cups chicken broth
	Salt and pepper to taste

Rinse the rice thoroughly with cold water until the water runs clear. Melt the butter in a covered saucepan over medium heat. Add the shallot, ginger, carrot, and crushed fennel seeds. Cook for three minutes, stirring occasionally, until the vegetables soften. Add the rice and stir to coat the grains with butter. Add the wine and cook until the liquid is reduced by half. Add the chicken broth and salt and pepper. Reduce the heat to a simmer, cover, and cook for 30 to 45 minutes, until the liquid is absorbed and the rice is tender. Remove from the heat and fluff with a fork.

Makes 4 servings.

ELKTROUT LODGE
Kremmling, Colorado

For the fly fishing purist, there is perhaps no better place on earth than Elktrout Lodge because of its unique combination of waters and conditions for dry fly trout fishing.

On the backside of the front range of the Rockies, Elktrout is tucked away on a plateau, in the shadow of a mountain, overlooking the Colorado River with the farm and ranch operations lining its banks. Within minutes of the lodge are ten miles of private streams, from the deep and languorous Colorado, to the clear and rushing Blue River, and the small but challenging Troublesome Creek. These streams offer the finest and most consistent dry fly fishing anywhere in the world for trout up to thirty-three inches, from narrow willow-lined streams to expansive big water river fishing. There are also eighteen fertile farm ponds filled with thriving trout up to ten pounds. Perhaps because this is a working farm valley, the nutrients from the farmland encourage the remarkable variety of insect life that supports such big, powerful, and healthy fish.

Part of the charm of the lodge is the evening meal where each night guests who have caught fish over twenty-one inches are presented with a pin designating their membership in Elktrout's 21 Inch Club. While this is a wonderful remembrance for guests, in truth it is not that difficult to do at Elktrout, and beginners routinely go home proudly sporting a 21 Inch Club pin. Slightly more difficult to get into is the Grand Slam Club—where an angler catches all four species of trout: brown, brook, rainbow, and cutthroat.

The lodge is the creation of Andrew and Marty Shepard and is a reflection of their desire to cater to visitors with the same grace and

hospitality that Marty and Andrew expect in their travels. The guides are all superior in their knowledge of the fishery and have the unique ability to challenge the expert and at the same time provide the beginner with a memorable experience.

Once the fishing is done, anglers relax in a beautiful log lodge, which is complimented by a unique outfitter-tent dining room, connecting the main lodge to the kitchen. After spending

a day in the rivers, a chair on the back porch perched on the bluff overlooking the valley is one of the sweet spots at the lodge. A good scotch and cigar can add to the tales of fish caught and even bigger fish lost.

This is a quiet, relatively unknown section of Colorado. Mainstream visitors pass it by without understanding the beauty of its quiet and rural nature. But anglers in the know understand that for the purest fly fishing experience in this country, with abundant hatches and massive fish, no other place can match the Elktrout Lodge.

HAWAIIAN PORK TENDERLOIN

- 3   cups pineapple juice
- 1   cup ketchup
- 3   tablespoons minced fresh ginger
- 1/4 cup sesame oil
- 6   cloves garlic, minced
- 1   cup soy sauce
- 1   cup firmly packed brown sugar
- 1   tablespoon ground black pepper
- 3   pounds pork tenderloin, trimmed

In a medium mixing bowl combine the pineapple juice, ketchup, ginger, sesame oil, garlic, soy sauce, brown sugar, and pepper. Place the whole cleaned pork tenderloin in the marinade and let it rest for several hours in the refrigerator.

Preheat the grill to medium heat. Remove the pork from the marinade and discard the marinade. Grill the pork over medium heat for 20 to 25 minutes or until a meat thermometer inserted in the center registers 145°, turning often to protect from over scorching and to evenly cook throughout. Let the pork rest for 5 minutes before slicing.

Makes 6 servings.

DUNGENESS CRAB CAKES

- 4 to 5 pounds Dungeness crabmeat
- 3   cups panko bread crumbs
- 2   small onions, diced
- 1   small bunch green onions, chopped
- 2   cups shredded cheddar cheese
- 1/2 cup Dijon mustard
- 2   tablespoons minced fresh garlic
- 1   tablespoon ground black pepper
- 1   tablespoon Spanish paprika
- 2   tablespoons dry sherry
-      Mayonnaise
-      Fresh chives for garnish
-      Lemon and lime slices for garnish

Mix together the crab, bread crumbs, onions, green onions, cheese, mustard, garlic, pepper, paprika, and sherry in a mixing bowl. After well blended, add enough mayonnaise to bind the mixture together just enough to form into cakes.

Heat a large skillet over medium-high heat. Shape the crab mixture into 10 to 12 cakes. Sauté the cakes in a small amount of butter in the hot skillet. Garnish with fresh chives and lemon and lime slices.

Makes 10 to 12 servings.

BANANAS FOSTER

1   cup (2 sticks) butter
1/2 cup firmly packed brown sugar
      Brandy
3   Bananas, sliced
      Vanilla ice Cream

In a medium pan, melt the butter over medium heat. Add the brown sugar, stirring constantly until dissolved.

When the ingredients have combined and the mixture is very hot, carefully deglaze the pan with 1 tablespoon of brandy. Add the bananas and cook for 1 minute. Scoop the ice cream into bowls and spoon the warm mixture over the ice cream.

Note: Other fruits can be used as well, such as apples, pears, mango, or peaches.

Makes 6 to 8 servings.

FIREHOLE RANCH
West Yellowstone, Montana

There is something to be said for "older." For more than 60 years Firehole Ranch has resided on the shores of Hebgen Lake, dead center in the heart of the most famous fly fishing area of the world. Within striking distance are the Madison River, the Yellowstone River, the Gallatin River, and the Henry's Fork of the Snake. There could not possibly be a fishing destination more steeped in the history and lore of western American fly fishing than here.

The lodge and its outbuildings are older, but everything is impeccably maintained. The history of its years on this lake and the old world craftsmanship that went into building it seem to permeate the lodge and its cabins. Maintaining that feeling is the unmatched service for which Firehole Ranch is so renowned. A one-to-one ratio of staff to guests makes possible superior attention to detail, down to every guest being known to the staff before even reaching the lodge and being immediately greeted on a first-name basis as if he had been there numerous times before. Favorite cocktails are remembered and each guest is treated as if he were the only guest in the lodge—a feat of remarkable staff discipline and pride. A return rate of over eighty-five percent is indicative of the quality of the service at Firehole Ranch.

The lodge sits in a meadow facing west to Hebgen Lake on 660 acres bordering the lake and the Gallatin National Forest. Early morning risers are generally treated to a moose wandering to the water's edge. After a day of fishing these great rivers, guests can sit back and watch the sunset over the lake while enjoying hors d'oeuvre and cocktails on the main patio. Each morning, the guests are ferried over the lake where they meet their guides and are then taken to the many cathedrals of fly fishing that are just a short distance away. The Madison and the Henry's Fork vie for the title of the most famous trout rivers in the world. Yellowstone Park with the upper Madison, the Gibbon, the Lamar, Slough Creek, and the Yellowstone are easily accessed. Hebgen Lake during prime time offers trout fishing for "gulpers," huge trout who gulp insects on the surface and can be a delight to anglers in a float tube that puts them right in the water with the fish.

For the trout angler who seeks the finest fishing in the world combined with service and cuisine that rivals any hotel in the world, Firehole Ranch is easily at the top of the list. Nothing escapes the staff's attention and when combined with the beauty of the location in the heart of Montana's Yellowstone country, it is hard to imagine a better place for the discerning sportsman who desires and expects the very best.

ROASTED QUAIL WITH ANDOUILLE AND SHRIMP STUFFING

Stuffing

2	tablespoons butter
1/2	cup minced sweet onion
2	garlic cloves, peeled and smashed
1/4	cup minced celery
1/2	cup chopped frozen spinach (thawed, with most of the water squeezed out)
2	andouille sausages, casings removed and cut into big pieces
1	egg
1/2	cup Parmesan
1/4	cup panko (or bread crumbs)
6	size 21-25 shrimp
1	tablespoon vegetable oil

Mustard sauce

1	tablespoon butter
1/4	cup diced shallots
1	tablespoon whole grain Dijon mustard (such as Maille)
1	tablespoon Dijon mustard
1	tablespoon maple syrup
1/2	cup white wine
1/2	cup chicken broth
1	teaspoon glace de viande
10	fresh sage leaves, thinly cut
1/4	cup cream
	Salt and butter to taste

Quail

4	semi-boneless quails (wing tips removed, patted dry)
2	tablespoons melted butter
8	wooden toothpicks, soaked in water
4	fresh sage leaves for garnish

For the stuffing, in a saucepan melt the butter over medium-high heat. Sauté the onion, garlic, and celery until golden. Add the spinach and stir. Remove from the heat.

In a food processor pulse together the andouille sausage, spinach mixture, egg, Parmesan, and bread crumbs.

Peel, devein, and cut the shrimp into pieces. Sauté the shrimp for 30 seconds the oil and toss into the stuffing. Cover and refrigerate.

For the mustard sauce, melt the butter in a stainless steel saucepan over medium heat and sauté the shallots, being carefully not to burn them.

Add both mustards and the maple syrup and stir well for 1 minute. Deglaze the pan with the white wine and reduce the sauce for 5 minutes.

Add the chicken broth, glace de viande, and sage and reduce for 5 minutes. Add the cream and cook over medium heat for about 5 minutes, or until the sauce has the desired consistency. Season with salt and pepper, if needed. Set aside and keep warm.

For the quail, preheat the oven to 425°. Stuff each quail with an equal amount of stuffing. Secure each end of the cavity with toothpicks (through the legs and where the neck was located). Brush with the melted butter and sit them breast up in a metal roasting pan coated with nonstick cooking spray.

Roast for 20 minutes. Turn the quail gently and cook for 10 minutes longer.

Remove the quail from the oven and wait 1 minute to remove the toothpicks. Pat dry. Spoon mustard sauce onto each plate. Top with a quail, breast up. Garnish with a sage leaf.

Makes 4 servings and 1/2 cup of sauce.

CHARBROILED BUFFALO TENDERLOIN

Yukon Gold Mashed Potatoes

2   pounds peeled and halved Yukon Gold potatoes
1   tablespoon sea salt
1   stick cold butter
1/2 cup warm 2% milk
    Salt and freshly ground white pepper

Cabernet Wine Sauce

1/3 cup chopped shallots
1 1/2 cups cabernet sauvignon
1/4 cup sweet vermouth
12 cracked peppercorns
2   sprigs fresh thyme
1   small bay leaf
1 1/2 cups demi-glace (made with 1 1/2 cups of
    boiling water and 3/4 ounces glace de viande)
    Salt as desired

Gorgonzola Butter

12 garlic cloves
1   tablespoon olive oil
2   sticks butter, room temperature
2/3 cup crumbled Gorgonzola (nice sized pieces)
1   tablespoon minced chives
2   tablespoons finely chopped Italian parsley
20 cracked mixed or black peppercorns
    Salt to taste

Buffalo

1   3- to 3 1/2-pound buffalo tenderloin, cut into six
    8-ounce steaks
    Olive oil
    Sea salt
    Pepper

For the potatoes, in a large pot cover the potatoes with water and sprinkle with the sea salt. Bring to a boil over medium-high heat and boil until tender and almost falling apart. Drain off the water.

Return the potatoes to the stove over low heat for a couple of minutes and beat the potatoes with a wooden spoon. Turn off the heat and mash the potatoes with a masher or through a food mill. Add the cold butter a little bit at a time and vigorously stir. Add the warm milk and lightly stir. Season with salt and white pepper. Keep a lid on the potatoes until ready to serve.

Note: Mashed potatoes can be made in advance. Keep them uncovered in a double boiler with a little milk on top. Stir again before serving.

For the wine sauce, place the shallots, wine, vermouth, peppercorns, thyme, and bay leaf in a stainless steel saucepan. Bring to a boil, then simmer on medium-high heat. Reduce the mixture by three-quarters. Add the demi-glace and gently simmer the sauce for 20 minutes. Strain the sauce through a fine sieve and keep warm until ready to use. Add salt, if desired. The thickness of the sauce can be adjusted by reducing it longer or adding a little water.

For the butter, preheat the oven to 425°. Sprinkle the garlic with the oil and wrap in foil. Roast the garlic for about 45 minutes or until soft. When the garlic is cool, mince and place in a mixing bowl. Add the butter, Gorgonzola, chives, parsley, peppercorns, and salt to taste. Using a rubber spatula, mix but do not over do it. Roll into a log shape and wrap in plastic or parchment paper. Refrigerate or freeze until needed. Bring the butter to room temperature when you are ready to use and slice to desired thickness.

For the buffalo, preheat the grill to high. Let the steaks sit at room temperature for 15 minutes before cooking. Brush the steaks with olive oil and put on a hot grill for about 6 minutes on each side for medium rare.

Set the steaks on a platter with a piece of Gorgonzola butter on top of each. Place in a warm oven while assembling your plates.

Place mashed potatoes on each plate and spoon cabernet sauce over the potatoes. Top with the buffalo steak.

Makes 6 servings.

BLACKBERRY BROWN BUTTER TART

Crust

1 1/2 cups all-purpose flour

1/3 cup confectioner's sugar

1/2 cup (1 stick) cold unsalted butter

Filling

10 tablespoons unsalted butter

1/4 cup all-purpose flour

3/4 cup sugar

2 eggs

2 teaspoons good-quality vanilla extract

1 pint fresh blackberries (rinsed and set to dry on a towel)

For the crust, preheat the oven to 350°. Process or mix with your hands the flour, powered sugar, and butter until crumbly. Press firmly into a 10-inch tart pan. Bake for 10 minutes and remove from oven. With a small metal measuring cup or the back of a spoon, press the crust gently back into shape. Bake for 5 more minutes and then cool.

For the filling, preheat the oven to 350°. Over low heat melt the butter in a small saucepan and continue to cook until golden brown and nutty smelling, being careful not to burn. Remove from the heat and let settle for 5 minutes. Skim the foam off and discard. Pour the butter into a glass measuring cup, avoiding the dark solids in the bottom of the pan. There should be 1/2 cup of browned butter, or just a little less. Cool until just warm. Combine the flour, sugar, and eggs in a food processor and process for a few seconds until smooth. Pour in the warm butter and vanilla and process again very briefly, just to blend.

Scatter the berries in the bottom of the tart shell. Spoon the filling over the berries and spread gently. The filling will spread as it bakes, covering the tart shell. Bake for about 50 minutes until set.

Makes 8 servings.

LONE MOUNTAIN RANCH

Big Sky, Montana

Writers and visitors who regularly stay at the magnificent Lone Mountain Ranch agree that the staff is the most accommodating and friendly of any resort in the country. Combine that reputation with the location, the historic ranch buildings, the proximity to Yellowstone, and the extraordinary number of activities, and one ultimate western experience awaits you.

Lone Mountain Ranch, which was placed on the National Register of Historic Places in December of 2006, is rich in the history of Montana. First homesteaded by Clarence Lytel in 1915 as a working cattle, horse, and hay ranch, it was sold in 1926 to a Chicago paper mill tycoon, Mr. Butler, and his daughter and son-in-law, the Kilburns. The Butlers built many of the existing buildings, sparing no cost in construction. Native lodgepole pine was used, and door hinges and locks were handmade. The reverse B bar K, as it was then called, was a showplace for Mr. Butler's extensive Indian artifact collection, some of which adorns the ranch's dining room and cabin walls today. The late newscaster Chet Huntley, along with Chrysler and several other large corporations, purchased Lone Mountain Ranch and much of what is now known as Big Sky Ski and Summer Resort and Meadow Village, in the late 1960s to develop one of Montana's first destination alpine ski areas. Current owners Bob and Vivian Schaap, natives of Wyoming, acquired Lone Mountain Ranch in the Spring of 1977 and since then have developed one of the most diverse and beautiful lodges in the Yellowstone area and the west.

Lone Mountain sits just a short drive from the Gallatin River, one of the great trout rivers that flow out of Yellowstone Park. The ranch's home waters read like a who's who of the great fishing rivers of the west: the Gallatin, the Yellowstone, the Missouri, the Madison, and in the park itself, the Firehole and the Lamar. One could live here for years and never touch all the water that Lone Mountain can offer.

One of the least known, but perhaps most wonderful, is the Lamar, a small river in the remote northeast corner of Yellowstone where most tourists don't venture. Flowing through the beautiful Lamar Valley, this untouched river valley is home to bison and a good number of the recently reintroduced wolf population. Stopping at a pull-off and walking just a few hundred yards, the world suddenly disappears

and you are alone in paradise. In September when the hopper fishing is on, there is perhaps no better place in the world for an angler to be.

Once the snows of winter arrive, the fly rods are hung on the wall, the cross country skis appear, and Lone Mountain becomes a mecca for wilderness skiers who can ski through a crystal forest with wandering herds of elk and bison for company. Lone Mountain has a history of greatness that remains undiminished and is a favorite of people all over the world who want to experience Yellowstone country with the people who love it best.

SOCKEYE SALMON GRAVLAX

1   3- to 4-pound salmon fillet
1   pound firmly packed brown sugar
1 1/2 pounds rock salt
1/2 cup black peppercorns
1/4 cup minced fresh thyme
1/4 cup minced rosemary
1   cup aquavit (Norwegian liquor)
     Diced red onion
     Capers
     Cream cheese
     Lemon wedges
     Rye crackers or toast points

Remove the skin and any fat and pin bones from the salmon fillet. In a small mixing bowl mix the brown sugar, rock salt, peppercorns, thyme, and rosemary. Place half the mixture in a square baking pan. Place the salmon fillet on top, making sure the entire bottom of the fillet is in the mixture. Pour the remainder of the mixture over the top of the salmon fillet, covering completely. Cover the pan with foil and place in the refrigerator for 24 hours.

After 24 hours remove the foil and pour the aquavit over the top of the fillet. Cover again and refrigerate for 12 more hours.

Slice the fillet very thin and accompany with diced red onion, capers, cream cheese and lemon wedges. Serve with rye crackers or toast points.

Makes 8 servings.

SPICY ASIAN DUCKLING

Dipping Sauce

1   cup hoisin sauce
14   ounces Guinness stout beer
1/2 cup apple cider vinegar
1/4 cup cornstarch
1/4 cup water
1   rosemary sprig
6   tablespoons crushed dry roasted peanuts
2   tablespoons chopped fresh cilantro

Duckling

1   4 1/2-pound whole duckling, skinned and de-boned
2   cups canola oil
     Salt
     Pepper
2   cups flour
3   eggs, beaten
7   ounces panko bread crumbs

For the dipping sauce, place the hoisin, Guinness, and vinegar in a saucepan and reduce by half. Mix the cornstarch and water and add to the sauce to thicken. Pour into a serving bowl and garnish with the peanuts and cilantro.

For the duckling, cut the duckling into six slices approximately 1 1/2 to 2 inches long. Cut any remaining duckling into slices. Pour the canola oil into a large skillet and heat over medium–high heat. Lightly season the duckling slices with salt and pepper. Dip each duckling piece into the flour, then the beaten egg, and then the bread crumbs. Fry in the hot oil until the duckling is golden brown on each side. Place the duckling on a tray lined with paper towels and place in a 150° oven to keep warm.

To serve, place the duckling on a serving plate and serve with the dipping sauce.

Makes 12 servings.

ALSATIAN
RED CABBAGE SLAW

1/2	pound bacon
1	head red cabbage, shredded
2	red onions, sliced
1	cup (2 sticks) unsalted butter
2	teaspoons thyme
2	teaspoons caraway seed
1	cup Dijon mustard
1/2	cup white wine vinegar

In pan sauté the bacon, cabbage, and onion over medium-high heat until soft. Add the butter, thyme, caraway, mustard, and vinegar. Reduce the heat to medium and simmer until the liquid is absorbed.

Makes 10 to 12 servings.

GRAN MARNIER MOUSSE
WITH HUCKLEBERRY SAUCE

Huckleberry Sauce

1	pound of fresh or frozen huckleberries
1/4	cup sugar
2	teaspoons Gran Marnier

Mousse

4	egg whites
	Pinch of salt
4	tablespoons sugar, divided
2	cups heavy cream
1/2	cup Gran Marnier
	Whipped cream for garnish

For the sauce, purée the berries with the sugar in the food processor. Stir in the Gran Marnier.

For the mousse, in a mixing bowl beat the egg whites and salt until soft peaks form. Add 2 tablespoons of the sugar until the whites are stiff. Set aside.

In another mixing bowl, whip the cream until stiff. Add the remaining 2 tablespoons sugar and blend in the Gran Marnier. Fold the cream into

the egg whites.

To serve, alternate layers of mousse and sauce in parfait glasses. Cool for 3 hours and garnish with whipped cream.

Makes 6 to 8 servings.

MADISON VALLEY RANCH

Ennis, Montana

ere someone to try to rank the greatest fly fishing rivers in the world, the arguments would be passionate and vehement, but there is no question that in the top two or three rivers would be the Madison. Whether to an expert angler who has fished all over the world or to a rank beginner, the Madison is one of the high cathedrals of trout fishing.

The Madison originates at the confluence of the Firehole and the Gibbon some twenty-three miles deep in Yellowstone Park, and from there it passes through west Yellowstone and becomes Hebgen Lake. Below Hebgen Dam it turns into another lake, this one created by a massive 7.1 earthquake that sheared off an entire mountainside and dropped it into the river valley: Quake Lake. This took place in 1959, which is quite remarkable when one realizes that this major geologic event happened within our lifetime. Below Quake Lake the Madison begins its run through the Madison River Valley—surrounded by some of Montana's most magnificent mountain scenery—until it meets the Gallatin and the Jefferson and creates the Missouri River.

On the banks of the channel section, a few miles below Quake Lake, lies Madison Valley Ranch. The channel section of the Madison is an intriguing part of the river because it is shredded by islands and channels as if the river were a rope and here unraveled into a number of separate strands. Whereas the Madison is traditionally fished from driftboats in the main section, here the angler is free to walk and wade through miles of riffles and pools. An angler could spend an entire week just poking around the channels in search of Madison River trout.

The lodge, on the banks of the river, is a simple walk from the channels or from Jack Creek, a small tributary of the Madison. Below the ranch the river comes back together and ambles its way through the valley surrounded by the jagged peaks of the Madison Range to the east and the Gravelly Range to the west.

Not only a great fishing lodge, Madison Valley Ranch offers some of the best bird shooting in Montana, in the lowlands of the Madison Valley. A wide and beautiful river bottom land valley that stretches to the mountain walls, these bottoms and hayfields hold a number of gamebirds and waterfowl that can be hunted in the fall, easily the most spectacular season in Montana. The combination of bird hunting in the morning and fishing in the afternoon,

surrounded by nature's beauty, is something any sporting person would find irresistible.

After a day spent in the outdoors, the chance to come back to a meal from world-class chef Scott Warren is a fitting end to the day. Using the finest local ingredients as well as imported mainstays, Scott sets a table that ranks at the top of lodge cuisine anywhere in the world. In his sixth year, he has created a reputation for the lodge that, along with the extraordinary sporting opportunities and the magnificent Montana scenery, is a very hard combination to ignore.

PARMESAN CRUSTED SEA SCALLOPS

Roasted Lemon & Chive Sauce

2   teaspoons olive oil

2   shallots, finely chopped

1   teaspoon minced garlic

3   cups dry white wine

    Zest and juice of 2 lemons, halved and charred on the grill

2   bay leaves

3   parsley stems

3   thyme sprigs

12 whole peppercorns

1 1/2 pounds (6 sticks) butter, room temperature

2   tablespoons chopped chives

    Salt to taste

    2-inch chive pieces for garnish

    Additional charred lemon zest for garnish

Sea Scallops

2   cups bread crumbs

1/2 cup shredded Parmesan

2   tablespoons chopped Italian parsley

2   pounds (approximately 24) fresh large scallops

1   cup all-purpose flour, seasoned with salt and pepper

2   eggs, lightly beaten

1/4 cup (1/2 stick) butter

2   tablespoons vegetable oil

For the sauce, heat the olive oil in a medium sauté pan and add the shallots and garlic. Cook for 1 minute. Add the wine, lemon juice, bay leaves, parsley stems, thyme sprigs, and peppercorns. Cook for 15 to 20 minutes or until most of the liquid has evaporated. When 1/2 cup of the liquid remains, remove the pan from the heat and whisk in the butter until it is completely incorporated.

Strain the sauce, then stir in 2 teaspoons lemon zest and the chives. Season with salt to taste. Keep covered and warm until ready to use. Do not keep over heat or the sauce will break down.

For the scallops, preheat the oven to 400°. Mix together the bread crumbs, Parmesan, and parsley in a bowl. Clean and pat dry the scallops. Season the scallops with salt and pepper. Dredge one side of each scallop in the following order: seasoned flour, eggs, and bread crumb mixture. Set aside.

Heat a sauté pan with a mixture of butter and oil. Brown the crumb side of each scallop. Take out of the pan and put on a parchment-lined sheet pan, crumb side up. Continue with the rest of the scallops. Once all scallops are browned and on the sheet pan, bake for 3 to 5 minutes.

To serve, place two crusted scallops on a warm plate and ladle 2 tablespoons of sauce around the plate. Garnish with 2-inch chive pieces and additional lemon zest.

Makes 12 servings.

CITRUS CURD AND FRESH BERRY TARTLETS

Pastry Dough

3 3/4 cups all-purpose flour

3/4 cup sugar

    Pinch of salt

1 1/2 cups (3 sticks) cold unsalted butter, cubed

2 tablespoons cream

3 egg yolks

3 cups dried beans (for weighting pastry while baking)

Filling

12 whole eggs

12 yolks

2 cups citrus juice (a mixture of the juice of 2 lemons, 1 lime, 1 grapefruit, and 1 orange)

2 cups unsalted butter, softened

2 cups sugar

3/4 cup black currants, divided

Raspberry-Ginger Coulis

24 ounces frozen raspberries

6 tablespoons sugar

    Pinch of salt

1 cup water

1 tablespoon minced fresh ginger

1 tablespoon lemon juice

For the pastry dough, preheat the oven to 375°. Sift the flour, sugar, and salt into a bowl. Cut the butter into the flour mixture until it resembles course meal (you may use food processor). Sprinkle in the cream and egg yolks and stir until the mixture just holds together. Wrap in plastic and refrigerate for 1 hour.

Roll out the dough on a lightly floured surface. Press into three 1/2-inch tart pans. Prick the bottoms of the pans with a fork and freeze for 10 minutes. Line the bottom of the tart pans with parchment paper or foil and fill with the dried beans. Bake the tarts for 10 minutes. Remove the beans and bake for 10 minutes longer. Remove the tarts from the oven and cool on a wire rack. When cool, remove the tart shells from the pan.

Note: Baking times may vary slightly, so watch for a golden brown color.

For the filling, whisk together the eggs, egg yolks, and citrus juice in the top of a double boiler over medium-high heat. Add the softened butter and sugar and stir constantly for 15 to 20 minutes, until the mixture thickens. Strain the warm mixture and refrigerate about 2 hours, until cooled. Stir in 1/2 cup of black currants. Fill the tart shells with the filling, reserving any remaining filling for assembly.

For the coulis, combine the raspberries, sugar, salt, water, ginger, and lemon juice in a deep pot and cook on low heat for 30 minutes. Purée the mixture in a blender or food processor. Strain through a fine-mesh sieve, pressing firmly with a rubber spatula. Taste, and stir in a little more sugar or lemon juice as needed. Place 1 teaspoon of the reserved filling on a plate. Arrange a filled tart on top of the filling and ladle the raspberry-ginger coulis around the plate.

Makes 12 servings.

ROASTED PHEASANT AND SMOKED BACON SALAD

12	strips high-quality smoked bacon
	Olive oil for drizzling
24	grape tomatoes, halved
1	tablespoon minced shallots
1	teaspoon minced garlic
6	tablespoons tarragon vinegar
1	tablespoon whole grain mustard
1	cup plus 2 tablespoons olive oil
1	tablespoon chopped fresh tarragon
	Salt and pepper to taste
16	cups assorted mesclun greens
6	6-ounce pheasant breasts, roasted and sliced
12	ounces aged white cheddar cheese, shaved

Preheat the oven to 375°. Line a sheet pan with parchment paper. Place the strips of smoked bacon on the pan and bake until done, approximately 12 to 15 minutes. Drain, cool, and chop. Set aside.

Reduce the oven to 325°. Line another sheet pan with parchment paper and drizzle with olive oil. Place the halved grape tomatoes, seed side up, on the pan. Bake in the oven for approximately 1 hour or until desired doneness.

In a blender combine the shallots, garlic, tarragon vinegar, and whole grain mustard. Turn blender on low and slowly add the olive oil. When emulsified, pour into a large bowl. Stir in the chopped tarragon and salt and pepper to taste. Adjust the consistency as desired.

Gently toss the assorted mesclun greens with the vinaigrette. Arrange the greens on a chilled plate and top with the pheasant, smoked bacon, baked grape tomatoes, and cheddar cheese.

Makes 12 servings.

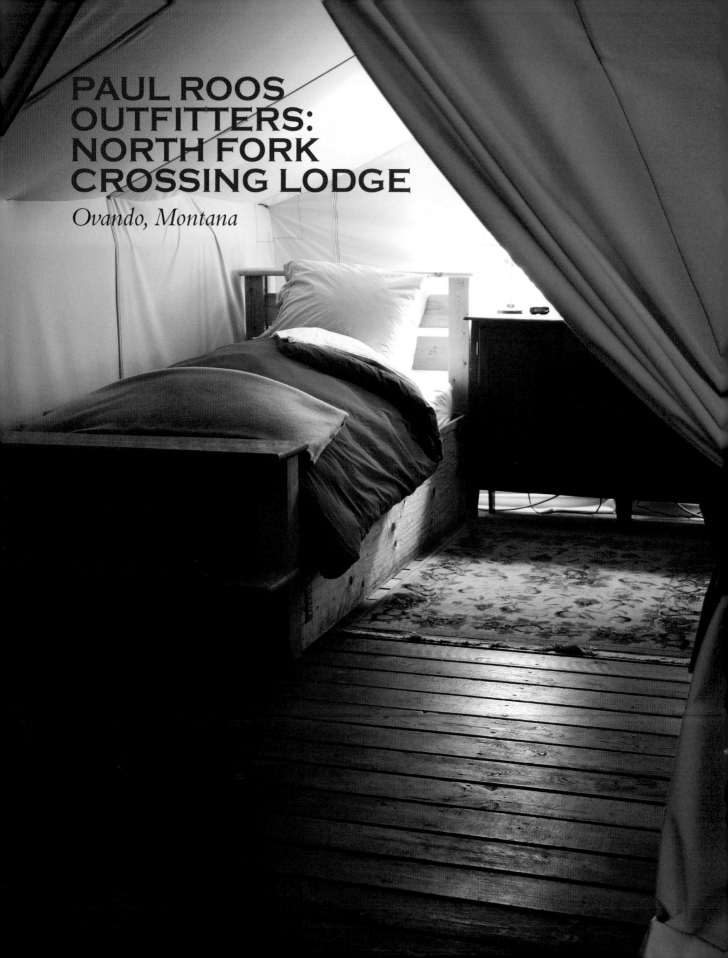

PAUL ROOS OUTFITTERS: NORTH FORK CROSSING LODGE

Ovando, Montana

When a legendary guide leads an adventure on a legendary river, generally the experience becomes its own legend. Such it is with North Fork Crossing Lodge, the vision of Paul Roos, one of the most respected guides in the western United States, and his home waters of the Blackfoot, a wonderful river elevated to legendary status by Norman Maclean in *A River Runs Through It*.

Things were not always beautiful on the Blackfoot. For a time the river and its tributaries and spawning habitats were ruined by indiscriminate cattle grazing and gold mine runoff. Roos worked tirelessly for years with Trout Unlimited and local ranchers to return the Blackfoot and its tributaries to their former glory. The once beleaguered Blackfoot now rivals the great rivers of southwestern Montana. North Fork Creek was one of these tributaries and it was here Roos established his unique vision for a lodge.

The North Fork Crossing Lodge cabins are walled outfitter tents scattered along the banks of the creek. Canvas, yes, but their wood floors, screened windows, and down comforters make a night in the wilderness an insomniac's dream cure. If you can't sleep here with the wind rustling the canvas and the cold held at bay by layers of down, there is no hope.

Now owned by Dana Post, the chef and a graduate of Denver's School of Culinary Arts, and Brian Boedecker, one of the lodge's guides, the lodge has retained Roos's vision of providing what might be the ultimate comfortable wilderness experience. In addition to float fishing the Big Blackfoot River, North Fork Crossing offers access to dozens of smaller, less familiar streams, lakes, and private spring creeks, plus secluded, unfloatable sections of nearby rivers. Day trips are also provided to the Mighty Mo—the Missouri River—only an hour away.

A special trip, offered by only a few outfitters, permits floating and fishing down sixty-one miles of the Smith River on a five-day trip. One of the most sought after trips in the West, this is one of the great experiences of a lifetime; floating sixty-one miles down a river that sees very few anglers. The camping

is comfortable, the food spectacular, and the scenery and wildlife are breathtaking. The only tough part of the trip is when it's over.

There are epic stories in the West of destruction and redemption. The Blackfoot and its benefactor Paul Roos are one of these stories. A stay at North Fork Lodge allows you to benefit from Paul's work and spend time in a paradise born of his vision of saving his home river. There is no better way to fish a river than to fish it with one who loves it.

PAN ROASTED QUAIL WITH ORANGE, HONEY AND THYME SAUCE

8	semi-boneless quail
	Salt and pepper
2	teaspoons fresh thyme leaves plus several sprigs for garnish
1/2	cup honey, softened
	Juice and zest of 2 oranges
2	tablespoons butter
1/4	cup Triple Sec liquor
3/4	cup game or veal stock

Place the quail in a shallow baking dish and season with salt, pepper, and fresh thyme. Drizzle with the softened honey, orange juice, and orange zest and let marinate for at least two hours (overnight in the refrigerator is preferred).

Preheat the oven to 375°. Heat a stainless steel sauté pan over medium-high heat and add the butter. Remove the quail from the marinade and reserve the marinade. Sauté the quail to an even brown on both sides (approximately 3 to 4 minutes per side). Remove the pan from the heat and place it in the oven for 10 to 12 minutes. Remove the quail from the pan, tent with foil, and let them rest while the sauce is made.

Carefully deglaze the pan with the Triple Sec, scraping all the brown bits into the sauce. Add the reserved marinade and the stock. Simmer the sauce until reduced to a thin syrup. Adjust the seasoning with salt and pepper.

Serve the quail on a bed of creamy polenta, drizzling the sauce over the top, and with a fresh thyme garnish.

Makes 8 servings.

CINNAMON AND CUMIN ENCRUSTED LEG OF LAMB

1	boneless leg of lamb, trimmed of excess fat
	Salt and pepper
2	tablespoons whole cumin seeds
3	tablespoons cinnamon
2	tablespoons butter
1/3	cup blackberry brandy
1/2	cup Montana huckleberry jam
1 1/2	cups good beef stock
1	cup huckleberries (frozen is fine)

Preheat the oven to 350°. Lay the lamb flat on a suitable work surface. Season with salt and pepper and then the cumin seeds. Coat the lamb with the cinnamon. It is important to season with the cinnamon last. Using kitchen twine, tie the lamb at intervals into an even-sized roast.

In an ovenproof sauté pan over medium-high heat, melt the butter and brown the roast on all sides. Place the pan in the oven and roast until an internal temperature of 125° is reached. Remove the pan from the oven and let cool slightly.

Remove the lamb to a serving platter, tent with foil, and let rest for at least 20 minutes before serving.

Deglaze the pan with the brandy. Add the jam and beef stock and reduce until thickened. Add the huckleberries and season the sauce with salt and pepper to taste.

Slice the lamb thinly on the bias and serve with the sauce. Serve with whipped potatoes and fresh asparagus.

Makes 6 to 8 servings.

CHOCOLATE BREAD PUDDING WITH CARAMEL SAUCE AND BANANAS

Bread Pudding

10   ounces semisweet chocolate pieces

3/4   cup milk

1   cup heavy cream

1/2   cup sugar

4   egg yolks

4   large croissants, finely chopped
      Sliced bananas and strawberries for serving
      Ice cream for serving

Caramel Sauce

1   cup corn syrup

1   cup firmly packed brown sugar

1/2   cup butter

For the bread pudding, preheat the oven to 325°. In a double boiler melt the chocolate and reserve. In a medium saucepan combine the milk, heavy cream, and sugar. Bring to a light simmer. Add the melted chocolate and egg yolks, stirring constantly until the mixture has thickened and is cooked through.

Place the chopped croissants in a large mixing bowl. Pour the chocolate custard over the croissants and mix thoroughly. Spoon the chocolate mixture into six greased ramekins and place into a water bath. Place the water bath in the oven and bake for 15 to 20 minutes. Remove the bread pudding from oven and allow to cool completely. The bread pudding can be made ahead and stored in the refrigerator for several days or can be frozen.

For the sauce, in a medium saucepan heat the corn syrup and brown sugar until the sugar is fully dissolved. Stir in the butter until fully incorporated. Do not boil.

To serve, warm the bread pudding in the ramekins on a sheet pan in the oven for approximately 15 minutes prior to serving. Turn the bread pudding out of the ramekin onto a serving plate. Top with sliced bananas and strawberries. Ladle 1/4 cup of warm sauce and serve with ice cream.

Makes 6 servings.

CARROT GINGER SOUP

Soup

1   pound peeled and chopped organic carrots

1/2   large onion, chopped

1   quart good chicken stock

1   3-inch piece ginger, peeled and chopped

1/3   cup honey

1/2   teaspoon curry powder
      Salt and pepper to taste

Garnish

1   1-inch piece ginger, peeled and puréed

1/2   cup sour cream

1   tablespoon honey
      Salt to taste

For the soup, place the carrots, onion, stock, and ginger into a stockpot and cook over medium heat until very tender (about 1 hour).

Purée the carrot mixture in batches in a blender or food processor. Do not fill the blender more than three-quarters full and be sure to cover it with a towel when blending to prevent burning. Return the soup to the stockpot over low heat. Add the honey and curry, and season to taste with salt and pepper.

For the garnish, in a bowl mix the puréed ginger with the sour cream, honey, and salt to taste.

Serve the soup with a dollop of the garnish swirled into the middle of the soup.

Makes 4 servings.

SPOTTED BEAR RANCH

Flathead National Forest, Montana

They call it "the Bob." The Bob Marshall Wilderness in western Montana is named after Bob Marshall (1901-1939), an early forester, conservationist, and co-founder of the Wilderness Society. The Bob Marshall Wilderness extends for sixty miles along the Continental Divide and consists of 1,009,356 acres of roadless wilderness. Add the adjoining Scapegoat and Great Bear Wildernesses and there are a total of 1,535,352 acres created by the Wilderness Act in 1964.

The Bob is the second-largest wilderness in the lower forty-eight states after the Frank Church River of No Return Wilderness in Idaho. In addition to numerous waterfalls, lakes, and dense forests, the wilderness is also prime grizzly bear habitat, and the U.S. Forest Service claims that the population density of this species is higher here than anywhere else in the United States outside of Alaska.

At the north end between the Bob and Glacier National Park lies Spotted Bear Ranch, one of the great fishing destinations in the lower forty-eight states. The reasons for its greatness are the remarkable inaccessibility of its waters to the general public and that it is home to one of the strongest populations of the aggressive westslope cutthroat trout, a threatened species that can be caught here under special conditions and regulations. The fact that this can be done with dry flies during the summer makes it all the more spectacular. Add huge bull trout, and you have a wilderness fishing adventure that is second to none.

The lodge is very secluded and comfortable with six private guest cabins, each with Three

Dog Down comforters and pillows which make for a great night's sleep after a day of the some of the world's best fishing. Because the wilderness allows nothing mechanized, the ranch's hallmark backcountry adventures are by horseback. Anglers ride for miles into the unspoiled country and fish rivers and streams for cutthroat, camping along the way. The trip is finished with a two-day float of about 17 miles

down the south fork of the Flathead River, often recognized as one of the greatest and most inaccessible trout rivers in the country.

While the Spotted Bear is very comfortable and the amenities are excellent, this adventure is not for the faint of heart. This adventure is for those who want to see what the world looked like and what the fishing was like before mankind stepped into the picture. The wildlife is right there with you, the scenery is breathtaking, and the memories will not be of spas and luxurious rooms, but of extraordinary quiet, pools of trout in pristine rivers that emanate from one of the great wilderness areas of North America and are untouched by pollution and the hand of man.

SLOW ROASTED DUCK

2 whole frozen ducks
1 8-ounce can frozen orange juice concentrate, slightly thawed
   Salt and pepper to taste
2 quarts water

Apple Cornbread Stuffing

1 1/2 cups cornmeal
2 1/2 cups whole milk
2 cups all-purpose flour
2/3 cup sugar
1 tablespoon baking soda
1 teaspoon salt
1/2 cup vegetable oil
3 eggs
1/4 cup butter
2 Granny Smith apples, diced
1 cup orange juice
1/2 cup firmly packed brown sugar

Huckleberry Glaze

8 ounces huckleberry jam
1/4 cup water
1 tablespoon butter

For the ducks, preheat the oven to 225°. Place the frozen ducks on a rack in a roasting pan. Rub the orange juice concentrate on all sides of the ducks and sprinkle with salt and pepper. Pour the water into the pan and place in the oven, uncovered. Cook for 6 to 8 hours or until an internal meat thermometer reaches 165°, basting every 2 hours and turning the ducks after 3 hours. Remove the pan from the oven and place in the refrigerator for 2 hours or more to cool.

While the ducks are chilling, prepare the stuffing. Preheat the oven to 400°. Mix the cornmeal and milk in a bowl and let stand for 10 minutes. In a large bowl, whisk together the flour, sugar, baking soda, and salt. Stir in the cornmeal and milk mixture. Add the oil and eggs and whisk until the mixture is smooth and free of lumps. Pour the mixture into a greased 13x9-inch baking pan and bake for 30 minutes.

While the cornbread is baking, melt the butter in a small saucepan. Add the apples to the melted butter and cook over medium heat until the apples are partially cooked.

When the cornbread is finished baking, remove from the pan and crumble into a mixing bowl. Add the cooked apples, orange juice, and brown sugar. Mix together until the cornbread is moist.

When the ducks have chilled, preheat the oven to 425°. Place the ducks on a cutting board and carefully cut them in half lengthwise. Remove all innards, backbone, and rib bones. Fill the duck halves with stuffing.

With the stuffing side down, place the ducks onto a greased baking pan and roast for 25 minutes or until the ducks reach an internal temperature of 160°.

For the glaze, in a small saucepan heat the jam and water over low heat. Bring to a simmer and add the butter. Stir constantly until the butter is fully blended.

To serve, spoon the Huckleberry Glaze over the ducks.

Makes 4 servings.

FLOURLESS CHOCOLATE TORTE WITH CRÈME ANGLAISE

Chocolate Torte

1   pound semisweet chocolate
1/2 cup water
2   cups sugar, divided
1 1/2 cups melted unsalted butter
6   eggs
2   cups heavy cream

Crème Anglaise

1   cup heavy cream
2   tablespoons vanilla
5   egg yolks
1/2 cup sugar

For the torte, preheat the oven to 350°. Grease one 10-inch round pan. Melt the chocolate in a double boiler over medium heat. In a small saucepan, heat the water and 1 1/4 cups of the sugar together until it reaches a boil and the sugar has dissolved. When the chocolate has melted completely, add the butter and the sugar mixture.

In a small bowl, beat the eggs, cream, and the remaining 3/4 cup of sugar together. Fold the egg mixture into the chocolate and pour into the prepared 10-inch pan. Place the pan into the oven. Bake for 35 minutes or until a toothpick inserted in the center comes out clean.

For the crème anglaise, in a small saucepan, bring the cream and vanilla to a light simmer. In a large mixing bowl, beat the eggs and sugar until smooth. Add half of the cream to the egg and sugar mixture and stir constantly until completely combined. Slowly add the cream and egg mixture to the remaining cream. Stir constantly over low heat. Remove from the heat when the sauce is slightly thick.

To serve, spoon the crème anglaise over the torte.

Makes 12 servings.

FRENCH ONION SOUP AU GRATIN

2   tablespoons butter
4   yellow onions, thinly sliced
1/4 cup brandy
1   tablespoon ground pepper
1   50-ounce can beef consommé
2   tablespoons dried thyme
3   bay leaves
1   French baguette sliced on a bias about 1/4-inch thick and toasted
6   slices Swiss cheese

Preheat the oven to 350°. In a large saucepot, melt the butter over medium heat. Add the onions and sauté until golden brown and caramelized, about 20 minutes. When the onions have turned golden brown, add the brandy and pepper. Be careful when adding the brandy as it may flame. Continue to cook the onions with the brandy for 3 minutes. Add the consommé, thyme, and bay leaves and bring to a simmer. Simmer for 15 minutes.

Ladle the soup into oven-safe soup bowls. Place one baguette slice on top of the soup in each bowl. Top each serving with one slice of Swiss cheese. Place the bowls on a cookie sheet and place in the oven. Bake for 15 minutes.

Makes 6 servings.

THE BLUE DAMSEL
ON ROCK CREEK

Clinton, Montana

Imagine walking up the grand log staircase in a Montana fishing lodge and having a stream of hand-carved trout in the handrail follow you upstairs or taking a shower next to a school of trout dancing along the wall on hand-painted Italian tile. Or imagine a classically trained violinist who happens to be a classically trained chef as well. Welcome to the Blue Damsel Lodge. The name seems appropriately beautiful for a lodge of such artistic detail and would fit even if a blue damsel weren't such a tasty insect from a trout's point of view and therefore such an excellent part of the pattern in the western Montana fishery.

The Blue Damsel Lodge building was the vision of an Italian artist and his wife who labored for three years. Each log was handpicked and hand-laid by the artist. The building is a work of art and the attention to detail is apparent, with the artist doing all of the work himself and trusting no one other than his wife to help. At each stage of construction, his wife added her work to the lodge: hand-painted murals, hand-carved trout in the banisters, hand-painted and fired tiles in all the baths, the kitchen, the bedroom fireplaces, and the floor downstairs.

Blue Damsel was a bed-and-breakfast until 2004 when Keith Radabaugh, a veteran of twenty years of adventure fly fishing travel, led a group of investors to search for a premier location and develop a lodge in the famous four rivers area of western Montana near the storied waters from *A River Runs Through It*, Norman Maclean's seminal work of fly fishing and coming of age in the west in the early twentieth century.

The four rivers area consists of four very different prime trout rivers that converge just east of Missoula. World-renowned Rock Creek and the legendary Big Blackfoot converge with the Clark Fork of the Columbia just east of Missoula. Then the Bitterroot's confluence with the Clark Fork is at west Missoula. This west slope headwater of the Columbia drainage has almost 400 miles of floatable trout-rich water, with prolific hatches and all wild trout: rainbows, browns, brook, and native westslope cutthroat, as well as a relative abundance of the protected, native "canary in the mine" bull trout.

The lodge sits on Rock Creek and looks upward to the Sapphire Mountains where elk and moose regularly wander across the meadows and eagles and osprey sail the skies above the lodge. After hours of fishing, the best part of the day is just getting started. Chef Josh Wing presents a spectacular table and then he and Keith entertain the guests with stringed instruments from classical violin to guitar and mandolin around the firepit.

Blue Damsel is aptly named for it is beautiful, artful, sophisticated setting—and the fishing isn't too bad either. For those who understand graciousness and superb attention to detail, the Blue Damsel Lodge is a wonderful choice.

BLUE DAMSEL
GARDEN SALAD

Vinaigrette

1 1/2 cups jellied cranberry sauce
2   tablespoons corn syrup
3   tablespoons olive oil
3   tablespoons balsamic vinegar
2   teaspoons Dijon mustard
1   teaspoon cracked pepper

Salad

8   ounces organic salad mix (thoroughly washed)
1/4   cup dried cranberries
1/4   cup crumbled Gorgonzola cheese
1/4   cup diced crisply fried pancetta (or bacon)
1/4   cup chopped candied pecans
1/4   cup thinly sliced red onion
2   garden tomatoes, sliced

For the vinaigrette, heat the cranberry sauce and corn syrup in a saucepan over low heat for 10 minutes to make a syrup. In a bowl combine the cranberry syrup, olive oil, vinegar, mustard, and pepper and whisk together.

For the salad, portion the greens into 4 bowls. Add the cranberries, Gorgonzola, pancetta, and pecans, spreading evenly throughout. Dress each salad with 2 tablespoons of the vinaigrette. Top with a few slices of red onion and tomato.

Makes 4 servings.

GRILLED RACK OF LAMB

Lamb

1   free-range organic rack of lamb
    Kosher salt
    Cracked pepper

Sauce

1   cup chopped red onion
5   garlic cloves, minced
2   tablespoons olive oil
1   cup red wine
2   cups diced tomatoes
1   cup lamb or beef stock
2   tablespoons firmly packed brown sugar
1   tablespoon chopped fresh oregano
1/2 cup whole kalamata olives (plus 2 tablespoons of olive brine)
1/2 cup julienned fresh basil, divided
    Kosher salt
    Cracked pepper

Pilaf

1   cup chopped red onion
1   tablespoon olive oil
    Juice of 1 lemon
1   cup chopped fresh parsley
1/2 cup chopped dried apricots
1/4 cup toasted pine nuts
1 1/2 cups Israeli couscous
1 1/2 cups boiling water

For the lamb, trim the fat cap from the outside of the rib rack using a sharp boning knife with a flexible blade. Trim all the meat from between the rib bones. Trim away any silver skin from the meat and portion by cutting into chops, each with two rib bones protruding. Liberally sprinkle with salt and pepper. Wrap the rib bones in foil to protect from flame and set aside.

Note: Render the thin strips of meat from the ribs to make the stock for the sauce.

Rack of lamb is full of flavorful fat but this fat makes it very flammable. Heat the grill until very hot. Before adding the meat to the grill, turn the heat down to medium or medium-low. This will prevent flare-ups. Grill the lamb for 3 to 4 minutes per side until rare to medium-rare.

For the sauce, in a large saucepan sauté the red onion and garlic in the olive oil over medium-high heat until translucent. Add the red wine and reduce by half. Add the diced tomatoes, lamb or beef stock, brown sugar, oregano, 1/4 cup of the basil, and salt and pepper to taste. Simmer at medium-low for 20 minutes, stirring occasionally. The sauce will be thick.

Use an immersion blender or food processor to lightly purée. Add the olives and olive brine. Keep warm.

For the pilaf, in a saucepan sauté the red onion in the olive oil just until translucent. Immediately remove from the heat and add the lemon juice, parsley, apricots, and pine nuts. Set aside.

Add the couscous to the boiling water in a separate saucepan and return to a boil. Cover and remove from the heat. Let stand for 9 minutes.

To serve mix the couscous with the fruit and nuts. Immediately serve the lamb with the Israeli couscous pilaf, kalamata olive and tomato sauce, and slices of baby summer squash lightly sautéed in butter. Garnish with fresh basil.

Makes 6 to 8 servings.

SALMON ASPARAGUS BISQUE WITH MORELS

Stock

1	pound leftover lobster and shrimp shells and salmon bones
1	onion
3	celery stalks
1	carrot
3	garlic cloves
2	bay leaves
1	teaspoon black peppercorns
1	teaspoon thyme
1	teaspoon salt

Bisque

1/2	cup (2 sticks) butter
3/4	cup flour
1	tablespoon finely chopped shallots
2	garlic cloves, finely chopped
	Stock (see recipe above)
1	cup heavy cream
1/4	cup sherry
1	teaspoon paprika
1	teaspoon thyme
1	teaspoon oregano
	Salt and pepper to taste
1	cup thickly diced morel mushrooms (may substitute oyster, porcini, or chanterelle mushrooms)
1	cup 1-inch, diagonally-sliced pieces fresh asparagus
1	pound cooked chunked salmon
	Chopped chives for garnish

For the stock, rinse the shells and bones. Coarsely chop the onion, celery, carrot, and garlic. Put the shells, bones, and chopped vegetables into a large stockpot. Fill the pot with water to cover the ingredients by at least 1 inch. Bring to a boil, skimming the foam. Reduce the heat to low and add the bay leaves, peppercorns, thyme, and salt. Simmer for 1 hour or more. Strain through a wire mesh strainer into a large bowl. Set aside.

For the bisque, in a stockpot melt the butter and slowly stir in the flour to make a light roux. Cook over medium-low heat, stirring constantly, until light caramel in color. Add the shallots and garlic. Cook, stirring, until the shallots are opaque.

Increase the heat to medium and slowly add some of the stock to the roux and stir to the consistency of a thick gravy. Add the cream and enough of the remaining stock to bring the soup to the desired consistency. Add the sherry, paprika, thyme, oregano, and salt and pepper to taste. Stir until hot and bubbly. Add the mushrooms and asparagus. Continue stirring until the asparagus is almost cooked to the desired doneness. Stir in the salmon chunks.

Serve in a wide, shallow bowl garnished with chives and serve with fresh, hot bread and a chardonnay.

Makes 6 to 8 servings.

AUNT FRANCES'S CARROT CAKE

Cake
2	cups sugar
3/4	cup oil
4	eggs
1	small can crushed pineapple (drained, juice reserved)
2	cups plus 1 tablespoon sifted flour
2	teaspoons baking soda
1	teaspoon cinnamon
1/2	teaspoon salt
2	cups shredded carrots
1	teaspoon vanilla extract

Frosting
	Reserved juice from crushed pineapple
1	package cream cheese, softened
	Confectioner's sugar as needed

For the cake, preheat the oven to 350°. Grease and flour a 13x9-inch pan. In a mixing bowl cream the sugar and oil together. Add the eggs one at a time and mix on high. Mix in the pineapple, flour, baking soda, cinnamon, salt, carrots, and vanilla. Pour the batter into the prepared pan. Bake for 30 to 40 minutes and cool.

For the frosting, in a mixing bowl mix the reserved juice and cream cheese until smooth. Add confectioner's sugar until the frosting is the desired consistency.

Makes 12 servings.

THREE FORKS RANCH

Savery, Wyoming

olorado and Wyoming are two square states. No great rivers form their boundaries, but their mountains give birth to some of the great river systems of this country. It is these birth waters trickling down from high mountain snowfields that are the true cathedral of the trout. On the border of these two great states, at the birthplace of one of these great river systems, lies Three Forks Ranch.

The word *ranch* has now been used by developers to mean anything in the west over two acres. But Three Forks is a working cattle ranch in the grandest historical sense of the word and incorporates 200,000 acres at the point where the middle fork, south fork, and north fork all come together to form the Little Snake River.

In an arid land, Three Forks has the distinct advantage of lying at the base of the Sierra Madre Range of the Medicine Bow National Forest, on the southern border of Wyoming, just north of Steamboat Springs, Colorado. The melting snows from this range feed the sixteen miles of private river belonging to Three Forks, as well as more than thirty ponds and lakes filled with rainbow, brook brown, and native Colorado cutthroat trout.

With such a grand scale, Three Forks is able to have a significant impact on conservation and has successfully completed the largest privately funded stream restoration project in the history of the United States. This includes a protected habitat for the cutthroat, offering anglers the opportunity to fish for this great species in a catch-and-release fishery, unparalleled for cutthroats.

The lodge is spectacular and on a grand scale that matches the nature of the surrounding land. The service is impeccable and offers amenities that rival any resort in the country. The

difference is the opportunity for true wild trout fishing, great fall elk and mule deer hunting, with accommodations second to none.

A significant part of this is the cuisine prepared by Christine Drabnis, a graduate of the Culinary Institute of America at Greystone

and Napa. She learned her craft at other guest lodges in the Rockies and offers a wonderful regional table as well as exotic entrées to satisfy the palate of any guest. The angling and hunting experience at Three Forks Ranch is on a scale commensurate with the mountains that surround the lodge. The cuisine is no less spectacular.

PAN-FRIED RAINBOW TROUT WITH CORNMEAL PEPPER CRUST

1   cup cornmeal
2   tablespoons fresh ground black pepper
1/2 teaspoon cayenne pepper
    Salt to taste
1   10-ounce rainbow trout
2   tablespoons vegetable oil

Combine the cornmeal, black pepper, cayenne pepper, and salt in a bowl and mix well.

Rinse the trout with cold water and roll in the cornmeal mixture.

In a heavy cast-iron skillet heat the vegetable oil to medium-high and pan fry the trout, browning both sides, until the trout flakes apart easily. If cooking more than 1 trout, use a flattop griddle following the same method.

Makes 1 serving.

TUNISIAN EGGPLANT SALAD WITH FETA CHEESE

1   pound tuna
1   pound eggplant
1   green bell pepper, chopped
1   red bell pepper, chopped
4   Roma tomatoes, chopped
1   tablespoon chopped fresh garlic
1/2 cup olive oil
1/3 cup red wine vinegar
2   teaspoon dried oregano
    Salt and pepper to taste
    Juice of 1 fresh lemon
    Mixed baby field greens
    Feta cheese

Poach the tuna and chill. Peel and cube the eggplant and then lightly poach and chill. In a large bowl combine the bell peppers, tomatoes, and garlic. Add the olive oil, vinegar, oregano, salt and pepper, and lemon juice. Mix in the eggplant and tuna. Marinate all the ingredients for several hours, stirring often. Serve on mixed baby field greens and top with Feta cheese.

Makes 4 to 6 servings.

CHILEAN SEA BASS WITH OLIVE TAPENADE

Sea Bass

1   7-ounce Chilean sea bass fillet, skinned
1   lemon wedge for garnish
    Fresh herbs for garnish

Braised Spinach

2   tablespoons extra-virgin olive oil
1   tablespoon minced shallots
2   pounds fresh spinach
    Salt and pepper to taste

Olive Tapenade

3/4 cup chopped, seeded, and skinned tomato
2   tablespoons capers
1/2 cup chopped Spanish olives
    Juice of 1/2 lemon
1   tablespoon minced shallots
    Chopped fresh thyme and Italian parsley to taste
    Salt and pepper to taste
1   tablespoon extra-virgin olive oil

For the sea bass, preheat the oven to 400°. Place the sea bass on lightly greased baking sheet. Bake for 20 to 25 minutes or until done. Prepare the spinach and tapenade while fish cooks.

For the spinach, heat the oil in a skillet over medium heat. Add the shallots and sauté. Slowly add the fresh spinach and season with salt and pepper. Cook only until the spinach is lightly wilted. Do not overcook.

For the tapenade, combine the tomato, capers, olives, lemon juice, shallots, parsley, salt and pepper, and olive oil together and chill. The mixture should resemble a fine relish.

To serve, make a bed of spinach on a plate. Add the baked fish and top with the tapenade. Garnish with the lemon wedge and herbs. This particular dish is served with wild rice and buttered baby carrots.

Makes 1 serving.

TRIPLE CREEK RANCH

Darby, Montana

The image of Montana is generally one of rugged mountains, tumbling rivers, big trout, grizzly bears, and all the attendant wonders that Big Sky country has to offer. This is a rough-and-tumble state, with a robust reputation, but there are a few places where this magnificent environment can be viewed from a destination that rivals many classic European hotels and dining experiences.

Such a place is Triple Creek Ranch. A member of Relais & Châteaux, this incongruous oasis of pampered comfort lies in some of the most staggeringly beautiful country Montana has to offer. On the western border of Montana, perched on the side of Trapper Mountain, Triple Creek Ranch is an opus to fine living from which guests can sally forth to experience all that is Montana, from the world's best trout fishing to a cattle drive. At the same time they can spend the evening sampling the finest wines and dining on cuisine that rivals the best restaurants of Europe.

Triple Creek is an adult resort that caters to adult tastes. The lodge is a magnificent log structure on 600 acres, high above the valley. Guests stay in individual cabins that are really rustic suites with fireplaces, hot tubs, decks, and interior amenities that rival great hotels. Within the main lodge is an award-winning wine cellar, a state-of-the-art showroom, and a Wine Spectator 2005 and 2006 Award of Excellence. The beautiful glass-encased room, finished with handcrafted South American mahogany racks, greets guests as they enter the rooftop lounge. With a capacity of 3,000 bottles, the cellar is home to mature Bordeaux and classic vintages, as well as house wines, all stored at an ideal temperature of 55 degrees. Special vintner weekends are available where wine lovers are treated to seminars and tastings from specific vineyards. It's not a bad way to end the day after a cattle drive or a float trip down the Bitterroot River. If being pampered is necessary, a massage in front of your fireplace is easily accomplished.

The Bitterroot River, a freestone river with its headwaters at the upper end of the Bitterroot Valley, just west of the Continental Divide, flows north through the valley into the Clark Fork of the Columbia River, west of Missoula. It is about ninety-eight miles long including the east and west forks and offers blue-ribbon fishing for trout including rainbow, brown, and the beautiful westslope cutthroat. There have not been any fish introduced into the Bitterroot since the 1940s and all fish caught are wild. That in itself is worth the trip.

Triple Creek is extraordinary to say the least. Very rarely does one find such a blend of culture and wilderness so perfectly tied together. It is the best of both worlds and a compromise to neither.

MICROCRESS SALAD WITH SWEET CURRY VINAIGRETTE DRESSING

Salad
1   cup microcress (or mesclun greens)
1   tablespoon roughly torn fresh parsley leaves

Sweet Curry Vinaigrette
4   tablespoons olive oil, divided
1   small shallot, finely diced
1   garlic clove, finely chopped
1   teaspoon Madras curry powder
1   teaspoon white wine
1   tablespoon cider vinegar
1   teaspoon honey
    Salt and pepper to taste

For the salad, toss the microcress and parsley together in a salad bowl. Cover and keep refrigerated.

For the vinaigrette, heat a saucepan over medium heat. Add 1 tablespoon of the olive oil and gently cook the shallot and garlic until translucent. Add the curry powder and cook until fragrant. Deglaze the pan with the white wine, cider vinegar, and honey. Remove the pan from the heat. Slowly whisk in the remaining 3 tablespoons olive oil. Add the salt and pepper to taste. Cool to room temperature and toss with the greens and parsley. Add just a little more salt and pepper to the salad if needed.

Note: Microcress is baby watercress.

Makes 4 servings.

TRIPLE CREEK MONTANA CHILI

1   onion, diced
1   red bell pepper, diced
1   yellow pepper, diced
1   green pepper, diced
1   tablespoon granulated garlic
3   pounds beef (prime rib, tenderloin, NY), diced
2   tablespoons olive oil
1   tablespoon paprika
3   tablespoons chili powder
1   tablespoon salt
1   tablespoon black pepper
2   cups chili sauce
1   can kidney beans, rinsed and drained
1   can diced tomatoes

In a skillet over medium heat sauté the onion, peppers, and granulated garlic.

In a large pot brown the beef in the olive oil. Add the paprika, chili powder, salt, black pepper, chili sauce, kidney beans, and tomatoes with juice. Stir in the sautéed onion and peppers and simmer for 1 hour.

Makes two gallons.

LOCAL GOAT CHEESE SANDWICH WITH SMOKED TROUT

- 2 ounces goat cheese
- 2 sun dried tomatoes, chopped
- 1 teaspoon each finely chopped fresh chives, sage, parsley, and rosemary
- 1 ounce chopped smoked trout
- 2 tablespoons olive oil, divided
  Salt and pepper to taste
- 1 good quality baguette, thinly sliced
- 1 teaspoon butter

Place the cheese, tomatoes, herbs, trout, and 1 tablespoon of the olive oil into a mixing bowl. Using a wooden spoon or spatula, mix all of the ingredients together. Taste and add salt and pepper if needed. Spread the mixture on the slices of baguette. Make sandwiches with the baguette slices by placing 1 baguette slice on top of another slice; repeat with the remaining slices.

Heat a sauté pan over medium heat. Add the remaining tablespoon olive oil and the butter to the pan. When the butter starts to foam place the sandwiches into the pan. After a couple of minutes flip the sandwiches. Cook until golden brown. The cheese should just start to ooze from the sides. Drain on paper towels.

Makes 4 to 5 small sandwiches.

BAKED CHOCOLATE MOUSSE

- 5 1/2 ounces dark chocolate
- 2 tablespoons butter
- 2 tablespoons heavy cream
- 3 eggs (yolks and whites separated)
- 1 tablespoon sugar

Preheat the oven to 350°. Melt the chocolate and butter in a bowl in the microwave or in a double boiler. Add the cream and egg yolks to the chocolate and mix using a whisk. In a separate bowl, whip the egg whites to soft peaks, adding the sugar at the end. Carefully fold the whites into the chocolate mixture using a rubber spatula. Scoop the mixture into a buttered soufflé ramekin or a pre-baked tartlet shell. Bake for 5 to 6 minutes. The center will be liquid.

Serve hot with ice cream or fruit salad.

Note: Mixture can be made up to six hours before serving.

Makes 4 servings.

South

MOUNTAIN HOLLOW AND COASTAL MARSH

Blackberry Farm
Chetola Resort at Blowing Rock
Deer Creek Lodge
Grosse Savanne Waterfowl and Wildlife Lodge
Shoal Grass Lodge and Conference Center

BLACKBERRY FARM

Walland, Tennessee

In the land of the Cherokee, the oldest mountains in the world are worn smooth and covered with the deepest and most diverse woodland in the northern hemisphere. Majestic? Not in the sense of the Rockies, but in the mists of morning these mountains roll to the horizon like the North Sea in winter, gray and forbidding, yet beckoning the wanderer to disappear into the shrouded valleys.

In the foothills of these mountains, in the land of the Foxfire, where the Scottish Highlanders sought refuge from the Clearances that forced them from their home and re-established their mountain culture, Blackberry Farm rests on 1,100 acres facing the misty mountains. Just a short drive south of Knoxville, Blackberry Farm invites guests to experience quite possibly the finest lodging and cuisine in the United States. A bold statement, yes, but backed up by award after award . . . as the number-one small hotel in the United States, the number-one hotel for service in the United States, and, for the purposes here, a top-tier hotel in the United States for dining. Blackberry Farm has done this two years in a row according to the Zagat Travel Guide. And awards from Conde Nast, *Travel and Leisure,* and others simply add to the extraordinary reputation of this inn.

Sandy and Kreis Beall bought Blackberry Farm in 1976 and expanded the inn from nine to forty-four guest rooms and suites. Each is perfectly appointed and maintained by a staff with a remarkable reputation for service and hospitality, far beyond the expectations of even the most discerning traveler. Add to that the setting, the opportunities for sport and relaxation, and finally, the award-winning cuisine, and there is a reason for its rankings.

Executive Chef John Fleer, a cum laude graduate of the Culinary Institute of America in Hyde Park, New York, was Mary Tyler Moore's personal chef before moving to Blackberry Farm in 1992. Here he developed his Foothill Cuisine, a truly American cuisine that has taken him and Blackberry Farm to the top of the list for great American dining.

Fleer elevates the traditional staples of mountain fare to the highest levels of fine dining without losing the flavor and the tradition of the simple society from which they sprang. Pears, pumpkins, buttermilk, cornbread, grits and collards, cold milk and blackberries. Fleer's staples are as simple as the mountain folk they sustained, but now they are part of a unique cuisine that has no equal. These recipes will stand as favorites, particularly for those whose heritage is in the mountains of east Tennessee.

CAESAR SALAD SOUP

9   large garlic cloves, peeled

4   tablespoons clarified butter

1   cup cleaned and coarsely chopped leeks

1/2 medium yellow onion, coarsely chopped

2   celery stalks, chopped

1/4 cup all-purpose flour

1 1/2 quarts chicken stock (see following recipe)

1 1/2 teaspoons minced garlic

1   teaspoon cracked black pepper

1 1/2 teaspoons Dijon mustard

     Dash of Worcestershire sauce

1   cup shredded Parmesan cheese

1   head romaine lettuce, washed and torn

2   tablespoons lemon juice

     Kosher salt

     Croutons for garnish

     Thinly sliced romaine lettuce for garnish

In a large stockpot, heat the clarified butter over medium-high heat. Lightly brown the garlic in the butter. Add the leeks, onion, and celery and cook until soft. Stir in the flour and cook for 2 to 3 minutes to make a blond (light-colored) roux, stirring constantly. Stir in the chicken stock. Bring the stock to a boil, then reduce to a simmer and cook for 20 minutes.

Add the garlic, pepper, mustard, Worcestershire sauce, and Parmesan and simmer for an additional 20 minutes. Add the romaine to the soup and stir. Puree the soup in batches in a blender. Do not fill the blender more than three-quarters full and be sure to cover it with a towel when blending to prevent burning. Pour the puréed soup into another stockpot over medium-low heat. Add lemon juice to the soup right before you are about to serve it. Season the soup with salt and pepper to taste. Garnish the soup with croutons and thinly sliced romaine lettuce.

Note: This soup will hold its vivid green color for a short time. It is better to add the romaine and puree this soup closer to the time that it will be served.

Makes 10 servings.

POACHED EGGS WITH STONE-GROUND GRITS

Crayfish Gravy

1/4 cup (1/2 stick) butter

2   large red bell peppers, thinly sliced lengthwise

2   medium onions, halved and thinly sliced

14 garlic cloves, peeled and thinly sliced

     Salt and pepper to taste

2   tomatoes, peeled, seeded, cored, and chopped

1/4 cup seasoned flour

4   cups chicken stock (see recipe below)

2   tablespoons Worcestershire sauce

2   tablespoons Frank's hot sauce or Tabasco

1   pound fresh crayfish tails, backs removed, coarsely chopped

Chicken Stock

3   pounds chicken or chicken bones, cut up

2   medium onions, diced

4   celery stalks, diced

3   medium carrots, diced

1   to 2 garlic cloves, peeled

4   quarts cold water

1   tablespoon whole black peppercorns

3   bay leaves

1   small bunch of parsley stems

Cheddar Cheese Grits

4   cups chicken stock or water

2   teaspoons kosher salt

1   cup stone-ground grits

2   cups grated medium cheddar cheese

1/2 cup heavy cream

3   tablespoons butter

     Kosher salt and ground black pepper

Poached Eggs

16 eggs at room temperature

     Dash of salt

1   bunch thinly sliced green onions (cut diagonally)

For the gravy, in a large sauté pan melt the butter over medium heat. Add the peppers, onions, and garlic to the pan and stir, scraping the bottom of the pan with a wooden spoon. Season the vegetables with salt and pepper, cover, and cook for about 8 minutes, or until they start to become tender and brown. Add the tomatoes and cook another 8 minutes, or until the tomatoes and their juices have thickened. Add 1/4 cup of the reserved seasoned flour to the vegetables. Stir and cook for about 3 minutes or until any liquid is absorbed and the vegetables start turning a darker brown. Scrape the bottom of the pan with a wooden spoon to deglaze the pan and to give the sauce some color.

Gradually stir in the stock, again scraping the bottom of the pan with a wooden spoon. Add the Worcestershire sauce and hot sauce. Bring to a boil and then reduce to a slow simmer and cook for 30 to 45 minutes, or until the sauce coats the back of a spoon. Toss in the crayfish at the very end and cook for 1 to 2 minutes.

For the stock, wash the chicken thoroughly in cold water. Place in a large stockpot and add the onions, celery, carrots, garlic, and cold water. Bring to a boil, immediately reduce the heat to a slow simmer, and skim the fat that rises to the top.

Add the peppercorns, bay leaves, and parsley stems. Simmer slowly for 4 to 6 hours, uncovered, periodically skimming away fat off the top. Do not stir the stock at all. After cooking, strain through a fine-mesh strainer. A second straining through cheesecloth will result in an even clearer stock and chilling will cause any remaining fat to congeal at the top, making it easy to remove. This makes 3 quarts, 2 of which you will use for this recipe. The remaining quart will keep in the refrigerator for 1 week or in the freezer for 6 months.

For the grits, bring the chicken stock or water and salt to a boil in a heavy-bottomed saucepot. Whisk the grits in and turn down to medium-low heat. Cook the grits for 30 minutes, stirring often.

Add the cheddar cheese, heavy cream, butter, and pepper. Season with salt and pepper. Keep warm.

For the eggs, fill a large saucepot with about 3 inches of water and a dash of salt. Bring the temperature to almost a simmer, about 180°. Doing one egg at a time, crack an egg into a small bowl and lower the bowl into the water, letting the egg slide out. Repeat with three or four eggs or until the saucepan has as many eggs as it will hold without being crowded. Cover the pan and cook for 3 to 5 minutes, or until yolks are desired consistency. (Three minutes for medium-firm yolks and 5 minutes for hard yolks.) Remove the eggs from the pan with a slotted spoon. Continue cooking in batches until all the eggs are poached.

To serve, place a large spoonful of grits in the center of a large bowl. Generously ladle the crayfish gravy over the grits. Top the plate with two poached eggs. Garnish with the sliced green onions.

Makes 8 servings.

BACON-WRAPPED TROUT STUFFED WITH CRAWFISH

Stuffing

1	tablespoon butter
3/4	cup diced onion
3/4	cup diced celery
1/2	cup diced red bell pepper
1/2	teaspoon minced garlic
1/2	pound crawfish, cleaned
	Salt and pepper to taste
1/4	cup white wine
1/2	cup (1 stick) butter

Trout

8	8-ounce fillets trout, skinned
12	ounces thinly sliced smoked slab bacon
	Salt and pepper to taste

Preheat the oven to 350°.

For the stuffing, in a large saucepan melt the butter over medium heat. Sauté the onions, celery, peppers, and garlic until soft. Stir in the crawfish and cook until just done, about 5 minutes. Season with salt and pepper. Deglaze pan with wine, add butter, and cool mixture.

For the trout, lay the fillet on a cutting board and slice down the back toward the belly, then stuff with the crawfish mixture. Season with salt and pepper. Lay out the bacon strips side by side on a piece of parchment paper with the sides overlapping. Wrap the trout in the bacon. Sear both sides of the trout in a hot pan over high heat. Transfer to a baking dish and cook in the oven for about 5 to 7 minutes.

Makes 8 servings.

BUTTERMILK PIE

Pie Crust

1/2 cup all-purpose flour

1/2 cup White Lily flour

1/4 cup sugar

    Pinch of iodized salt

1/4 teaspoon baking powder

4   tablespoons butter, chilled

3   eggs, beaten

Filling

3/4 cup (1 1/2 sticks) butter, softened

2 1/4 cups sugar

4 1/2 tablespoons all-purpose flour

6   eggs, beaten

1 1/2 teaspoons lemon juice

1   teaspoon vanilla

2   cups buttermilk

    Whole nutmeg

For the crust, combine the all-purpose flour, White Lily flour, sugar, salt, and baking powder. Cut in the butter. Stir in the eggs. Knead the mixture until you are able to press it into a ball. Let the ball of dough rest for 1 hour in the refrigerator. Roll out the dough and place it into a 9-inch pie pan.

Preheat the oven to 375°.

For the filling, in a mixing bowl beat the butter, sugar, and flour until there are no lumps. Add the eggs, one at a time, beating continuously. Add the lemon juice, vanilla, and buttermilk. The mixture will look curdled, but that is okay.

Pour the buttermilk mixture into the unbaked piecrust. Grate nutmeg to taste over the top or sprinkle with ground nutmeg if you don't have fresh. Bake until set and lightly brown on top, about 45 to 50 minutes. The crust will puff up and may crack slightly, but that is normal. Rotate the pie in the oven after 30 minutes of baking. Serve at room temperature.

Makes one 9-inch pie.

CHETOLA RESORT
AT BLOWING ROCK

Blowing Rock, North Carolina

Chetola is Cherokee for "haven of rest." Aptly named, Chetola Resort lies just off the Blue Ridge Parkway in the mountains of North Carolina near a place called Blowing Rock. Before 1752, when Moravian Bishop August Gottlieb Spangenberg visited the Blowing Rock area, the windy cliffs were home to the Cherokee and the Catawba Indian tribes, hostile to each other. It is said that two star-crossed lovers, one from each tribe, were walking near the Rock when the reddening sky signaled to the brave that he must return to his tribal duty, and the maiden urged him to stay with her. His desperation in choosing between duty and love caused him to leap from the edge of the gorge toward the rocks below, while the maiden beseeched the Great Spirit to bring him back to her. The famous winds of the John's River Gorge blew her lover back into her arms, and this legend was born.

Blowing Rock has always been a resort. The high elevation was a welcome refuge from the heat of the southern summers, and people have been coming here for generations to enjoy the spectacular mountain scenery and the pleasing summer weather.

Chetola's story is one of a long line of owners, each adding their touch to its present estate-quality grandeur. It was originally purchased in 1846 by William Stringfellow, an Alabama banker, and then in 1926 by Luther Snyder, the Coca-Cola King of the Carolinas. Snyder refined the estate to one of the grandest in the region. Today Chetola is owned by Rachael Renar and her son Kent Tarbutton, who have gone even further in developing the resort with a keen eye of maintaining its beauty and paying homage to its storied past.

The Bob Timberlake Inn opened in 2004 in collaboration with one of North Carolina's most famous artists. Timberlake, who has spent his life painting and recording the fading rural nature of the Blue Ridge, is a remarkably successful artist and considered the master of the American Realist genre. Each room, named after a significant historical figure in Chetola's and Blowing Rock's history, was designed by Bob Timberlake using his own furniture designs based on his art. With Timberlake's help the manor house has been returned to the golden days of the 1920s when the Coca-Cola King entertained his guests in grand fashion.

Today, Chetola maintains its late eighteenth- and early nineteenth-century grandeur while offering an extraordinary number of activities for the guest including being the only Orvis-endorsed fly fishing lodge in North Carolina. Anglers can float or wade over 300 miles of small streams and rivers for brown, brook, and rainbow trout as well as smallmouth bass.

The Manor House Restaurant at Chetola pays homage to its history and serves a variety of menus with historical dishes from the region and its unique mountain culture. Unquestionably, Chetola is a visit to another time when life was lived on a grand scale and the mountains of the Blue Ridge called to heat-oppressed southerners and offered them a true haven of rest.

SHRIMP TARBUTTON

2 tablespoons butter

1 small shallot, minced

1/4 cup minced garlic

1/4 cup minced celery

1/4 cup chopped fresh parsley

6 ounces jumbo lump crabmeat

1 tablespoon mayonnaise

1/2 cup unseasoned bread crumbs

1/2 teaspoon Old Bay seasoning

    White wine if needed

12 large shrimp, peeled, tail on

6 strips apple-cured bacon, halved

    Hollandaise sauce for serving if desired

Preheat the oven to 400°. In a small sauté pan melt the butter and cook the shallot, garlic, celery, and parsley until translucent. Remove from the heat and add the crabmeat, mayonnaise, bread crumbs, and Old Bay seasoning.

Mix lightly until the mixture can be formed into small balls. Add white wine if more liquid is needed. Do not compress the mixture as it will become too dense. Form the mixture into 12 balls and place a shrimp around each ball. Wrap each shrimp with a piece of bacon and secure with a plain wooden toothpick. Bake until the bacon is done but not crisp. Top with hollandaise sauce if desired.

Makes 4 servings.

BLEU WEDGE SALAD

1   cup all-purpose flour
     Old Bay, Lawry's or other seasoning blend to
     taste
1   yellow onion, thinly sliced
     Vegetable oil for frying
1   head iceberg lettuce
12   ounces bleu cheese dressing
8   ounces quality crumbled bleu cheese or
     Gorgonzola cheese
1   pint grape tomatoes
     Chopped pecans

Combine the flour and seasoning mix in a bowl.
Toss the onion in the mixture until coated. Heat the
vegetable oil in a deep fryer or heavy-bottomed pan.
Add the onions and cook until browned. Set aside.

Cut the lettuce into 8 wedges and set each wedge
on a plate. Top with the dressing, bleu cheese
crumbles, and fried onions. Garnish with the tomatoes and pecans.

Makes 8 servings.

WHISKEY STEAK

Marinade
1/4 cup soy sauce
1/2 cup Jack Daniels (or other bourbon)
1/2 cup firmly packed brown sugar
1/4 cup minced onion
     Cornstarch and water (equal parts)

Steak
2 1/2 to 3 pounds steak (rib eye, tenderloin, flat iron,
     or London broil)

For the marinade, mix together the soy sauce,
bourbon, brown sugar, and onion in a bowl. Cover
and chill overnight.

In a small saucepan bring the marinade to a
simmer. Thicken slightly with the cornstarch
mixture. When heated through, strain.

For the steak, place the steak in a shallow dish and
add half of the marinade. Marinate in the refrigerator for 1 hour.

Preheat the grill and cook the steak until the
desired doneness. Heat the remaining marinade in
a small saucepan and serve with the steak.

Makes 6 to 8 servings.

DEER CREEK LODGE

Sebree, Kentucky

So what is it you want to do? Duck hunt? Doves, turkeys, trophy bucks, huge bass? Want to hunt upland birds behind Deer Creek trained dogs? Want your dog trained? Take your pick or do it all. Deer Creek offers all of this in one of the most comprehensive sporting lodges in the country. Just below the Ohio River in some of the best hunting country in the south central United States, Deer Creek is a remarkable combination of great hunting and extraordinary game management.

Deer Creek Lodge was borne of passion, dedication, and relentless determination. Legendary at first for its trophy whitetails and more recently for its acclaim as the first and only Orvis-endorsed wing shooting lodge in the state of Kentucky and the Orvis Wing Shooting Lodge of the year in 2006-2007, the history of Deer Creek's core property can be traced back to the 1840s. It was then that Captain James R. "Cap" Stull purchased a small parcel of land in the gently rolling hills four miles west of Sebree, Kentucky. Generation after generation accumulated additional parcels, and in 1978 the 365-acre core property was founded as a commercial hunting operation by Tim Stull, the club's manager and the great-great grandson of Cap Stull. Today Deer Creek Lodge offers more than 14,000 acres of pristine, private property to guests.

What's remarkable is the sheer volume of wild birds and that while offering spectacular hunts, the lodge also maintains the population. This is the core of who they are. As Tim Stull explains it, "We try and maintain 2,000 to 3,000 ducks on our refuge at all times. We have rest ponds on either end of our refuge, and our ducks are free-ranging. They can go anywhere they want anytime they want, but they still stay on our refuge. In a morning's hunt, you should see 1,000 to 2,000 ducks, all mallards, and you'll have one of the most fantastic waterfowl hunts you've ever had." For the addicted duck hunter a statement like this is staggering.

Finish a morning of duck hunting with thousands of ducks whistling by and then find yourself flushing 200 upland birds in an afternoon hunt and you've had an experience in

bird hunting that cannot be equaled anywhere in the world. This is bird hunting heaven.

Follow such a day with a stay at a 10,000-square-foot lodge with three-story windows looking out over the lake and the only thing left is the food. Chris Henderson, an award-winning chef from Australia, prepares spectacular food as he dances his way around the kitchen in a culinary display of joy that is something to behold.

Many lodges claim that no expense is spared to give the guest the best experience. In the case of Deer Creek Lodge, this is a fact. There is nothing like it in the world.

KENTUCKY CORN PUDDING

2   15-ounce cans corn, drained
4   eggs
3   tablespoons sugar
2   tablespoons all-purpose flour
1   teaspoon salt
1 3/4 cups whole milk
1/2 stick margarine

Preheat the oven to 350°. Place the corn, eggs, sugar, flour, salt, and milk in a blender. Pulse two times at high speed. Continue mixing until blended. Grease a deep-dish casserole with some of the margarine. Pour the blended mixture into the casserole dish. Cut the remaining margarine into the mixture and bake until the pudding is just set and light golden, about 45 minutes. Stir the casserole twice during the first 15 minutes of cooking.

Makes 6 servings.

MANDARIN AND STRAWBERRY SALAD WITH POPPY SEED DRESSING

Poppy Seed Dressing
1   cup olive oil
1/2 cup sugar
1/3 cup apple cider vinegar
1   tablespoon poppy seeds
1   tablespoon grated onion
1   teaspoon salt
1   teaspoon dry mustard

Salad
6   ounces mixed greens
1   11-ounce can Mandarin oranges, drained
1   cup sliced strawberries
1   cup Feta cheese (optional)

For the dressing, mix the oil, sugar, vinegar, poppy seeds, onion, salt, and dry mustard in a bowl and blend well.

For the salad, toss the mixed greens gently with oranges and strawberries in a large bowl. Sprinkle with the dressing and toss to coat. Top with feta cheese if desired.

Makes 4 servings.

VENISON BACKSTRAPS WITH GARLIC SAUTÉED MUSHROOMS

Backstraps
    Backstraps from 1 deer (or 1 whole beef or pork tenderloin)
12 garlic cloves, minced
    Cavender's Greek Seasoning
1   15-ounce bottle Worcestershire Sauce
1   cup extra-virgin olive oil
2   5-ounce bottles Pickapeppa Sauce or any Jamaican-style sauce

Garlic Sautéed Mushrooms
2   heaping tablespoons minced garlic
2 to 3 sticks butter
1/2 cup soy sauce (such as Kikkoman)
2 to 4 8-ounce packages fresh sliced mushrooms

For the backstraps, thoroughly clean and trim the backstraps or tenderloin. Be sure that all the ligaments and silver skin are removed. Rub liberally with the garlic, then sprinkle with Cavender's and pat into the meat. Cut the backstraps in half and place in a large stockpot. Sprinkle generously with the Worcestershire sauce, and then gently add the olive oil by holding a spoon directly over the meat and pouring the oil across the spoon. (The olive oil will wash off the Cavender's and garlic if you're not careful.) Pour the Pickapeppa sauce over the top of the backstraps. Do not stir. Marinate "as is" for 1 to 2 hours in the refrigerator (longer marinating will overpower the meat). Stir the meat with the marinade to cover thoroughly and let sit for an additional 30 minutes to 1 hour at room temperature.

Preheat a grill to medium. Remove the backstraps from the marinade and discard the marinade. Cook the backstraps over charcoal to the desired temperature. (Meat is best cooked no more than medium.)

For the mushrooms, in a saucepan over medium heat combine the garlic, butter, and soy sauce.

Heat until the mixture simmers, then add the mushrooms. Sauté the mushrooms to the desired texture. If you cook the mushrooms too long, they will wilt.

Note: For a very special treat, sear the backstraps over high heat, remove from the grill and wrap in bacon, then cook until the bacon is done. This takes a lot of time, but it is well worth the effort.

The above recipes are well complimented by wild rice, asparagus, and either candied carrots or a pineapple casserole.

Makes 4 servings.

GROSSE SAVANNE WATERFOWL AND WILDLIFE LODGE

Lake Charles, Louisiana

The Louisiana license plate motto is "Sportsman's Paradise" for a reason. Perhaps no where else can a sportsman find such a diversity of wildlife, with hunting and fishing opportunities such as those found in the southern marshes of Louisiana. The reason is water. Fresh and saltwater lakes, rivers, and marshes are nature's nursery and provide an incomparable habitat for an extraordinary range of species, both game and non-game. For the sportsman, this part of the world is indeed a paradise.

In the southwest corner of this paradise on 50,000 acres of managed Louisiana ecosystem is Grosse Savanne Lodge, an old-world Cajun experience that immerses the hunter and angler in the Cajun culture of living off the land and all of its offerings and the remarkably unique cuisine that's evolved over the past 200-plus years.

The Cajun culture originated from the 1755 deportation of French Acadians from Canada by the British, which was loosely documented by Henry Wadsworth Longfellow in his epic poem *Evangeline*. Settling in southern Louisiana, Cajuns adapted to the environment and became a breed of hearty watermen who made their way as fishermen, hunters, and trappers and created a culture so unique and isolated that in many places it remains relatively undiluted to this day.

Cajuns love a good time, and their food and music are distinctive hallmarks of their culture. It is this unique waterman's culture that surrounds visitors to Grosse Savanne Lodge, which is nestled in the heart of Cameron Parish (county). The largest parish in Louisiana, Cameron has twenty-six miles of natural Gulf of Mexico beaches, abundant wildlife, fisheries, and fresh and saltwater marshes. Fed by three river systems—the Sabine, Calcasieu, and Mermentau—750,000 of Cameron's 900,000 acres are defined as coastal wetlands, open

water or open range. Grosse Savanne encompasses more than 50,000 of the parish's wetlands, prairies, and agricultural fields, and is bordered by the finest saltwater lake in the state.

In the heart of this ecosystem is the lodge, a former private home built in the southern tradition of pier foundations, big rooms, bigger porches, and magnificent hospitality. From here hunters can access the bottom of the Mississippi flyway for ducks and geese in arguably the finest waterfowl range in the world. Millions of ducks and geese dump into this area as they make their way down the great central corridor of waterfowl migration. For any hunter stricken with the waterfowl addiction, it is the opportunity of a lifetime.

Where else can one hunt alligators, catch trophy bass in freshwater, and redfish and sea trout in saltwater? This is a true glimpse into the Cajun life and their undeniable skills as watermen who live with the land and pull their subsistence from it.

What is taken is eaten, and here the real fun begins. There is an old saying that Cajuns live to eat. Blended with a touch of Cajun spice, a drop of Creole sass, and the finest Southern ingredients, meals are from long-standing recipes that have evolved in this culture and are loaded with crawfish and shrimp, peppers and spices, meats and sauces.

This is a world unto its own—a culture true to itself and all the more remarkable for its purity. There are not many places like it left.

GROSSE SAVANNE'S BREAD PUDDING WITH RUM SAUCE

Bread Pudding

3   large eggs
1   cup sugar
1/2   teaspoon cinnamon
1 1/2 teaspoons vanilla
1/2   quart half-and-half
6 to 8 bread slices, torn into small pieces

Rum Sauce

1   stick butter
1   cup sugar
1/2   cup good-quality rum

For the bread pudding, preheat the oven to 350°. In a medium bowl, beat the eggs, sugar, cinnamon, vanilla, and half-and-half well. Add the torn bread and mix lightly. Pour into a 9-inch round cake pan that has been well buttered. Bake for 30 to 35 minutes or until golden brown. Remove from the oven and let cool. The pudding will fall somewhat as it cools; this is normal.

For the rum sauce, in a saucepan cook the butter, sugar, and rum over medium heat until the butter melts and the sauce is thickened.

To serve, slice the bread pudding into 8 pie-shaped wedges. Drizzle the rum sauce over each serving of bread pudding.

Makes 8 servings.

GROSSE SAVANNE'S SPECIAL SPINACH SALAD

1   5-ounce package baby spinach
4   hard-boiled eggs, sliced
1   small purple onion, thinly sliced
1/2   cup real bacon bits
1   1-ounce envelope Italian dressing mix (such as Good Seasons)
5   teaspoons confectioner's sugar

In a large bowl toss the spinach, eggs, onion, and bacon bits. Combine the dressing mix and confectioner's sugar in a container with a tight-fitting lid; mix well. Prepare the dressing by adding oil and vinegar to the container according to the dressing mix package directions. Shake well. Pour over the salad and toss.

Serve at once.

Makes 4 servings.

GROSSE SAVANNE'S PERFECT BEEF TENDERLOIN

1   4- to 5-pound beef tenderloin, trimmed
2   teaspoons seasoned salt (such as McCormick)
1   teaspoon coarse ground black pepper
1   teaspoon garlic powder
1   teaspoon ground red pepper

Preheat the oven to 350°. Place the tenderloin in a foil-lined shallow baking pan and season with the seasoned salt, black pepper, garlic powder, and red pepper. Place in the oven and roast until a meat thermometer inserted in the center registers 130°, 30 to 45 minutes. Remove from the oven and cover with foil and a dishtowel. Let stand covered for 15 minutes and then slice. The meat will be rare to medium-rare. For medium, cook 15 minutes longer.

Makes 8 servings.

SHOAL GRASS LODGE AND CONFERENCE CENTER

Aransas Pass, Texas

A few years ago the redfish's future was in doubt. This magnificent gamefish was so sought after for eating that it was in danger of disappearing, but thanks to the Coastal Conservation Association (CCA) the redfish is back and healthy. There is perhaps no better place in the world to go after this fish than Shoal Grass Lodge on the south Texas Gulf coast.

Reds are common now from North Carolina to Texas and are the premier inshore species of the Gulf, in particular to fly fishermen. There is perhaps no greater thrill than stalking the glassy shallows looking for the telltale signs of feeding redfish. Often their tails and sometimes even their backs are out of the water as they feed in remarkably shallow water. You can see nervous water where a school is moving, the sparkle of tails disturbing the surface, the push of a hump of water as a big red comes at you just a fraction of an inch under the surface. But your approach and presentation must be perfect or you will find yourself shaking your head as you watch a big red rocket off the flat as they are very wary.

If you are blessed to do everything right and one of these great fish takes your fly, you are in for an angling treat, as they are fast as lightning and, since caught in shallow water, have no where to go but out. Perhaps, though, what you will treasure most is the solitude and the quiet. The water is still, the sun is high and there is a blanket of quiet that is priceless these days.

Shoal Grass Lodge was built on one of the most beautiful sections of the Texas coast. Overlooking Redfish Bay in Aransas Pass, Texas, Shoal Grass has much to offer. Not only is the redfish in this shallow water haven, but speckled trout and redfish also inhabit the bay. Further out in the Gulf, there are cobia,

jacks, tuna, and billfish. There are not too many places where the options are so varied for the angler.

Then there are the ducks. Thousands and thousands of them. Every waterfowler wants to hunt the back marshes of the Texas coast, and Shoal Grass offers some of the finest. The experience is like being in a John Cowan painting; you'll certainly want to own one when you leave.

Shoal Grass is the complete Texas coast experience with a beautiful setting, offering almost everything a sportsman could ask for. The dining experience is pure Texas, with Texas beef, Texas seafood, and Texas hospitality. What better meal is there to come home to after a day walking the shallows in search of big red?

PAN-SEARED GROUPER WITH TROPICAL SALSA

Salsa

2 cups cubed mango
2 cups cubed pineapple
2 cups cubed papaya
1 cup diced roasted red bell peppers
1 bunch fresh cilantro, chopped
1 cup orange marmalade
2 limes, juiced
2 tablespoons diced jalapeños

Grouper

2 tablespoons olive oil
6 8- to 10-ounce grouper fillets
   Cajun spice for coating
   Mixed greens for serving

For the salsa, in a bowl combine the mango, pine-apple, papaya, roasted peppers, cilantro, orange mar-malade, lime juice, and jalapeños. Let the mixture sit while preparing the grouper.

For the grouper, in a cast-iron frying pan heat the olive oil until smoking. Coat both sides of the grou-per with Cajun spice. Place the coated grouper into the pan. Cook for 2 to 3 minutes per side (depend-ing on thickness), until done.

To serve, transfer the grouper to a serving dish, plac-ing on top of mixed greens. Spoon the Tropical Salsa on top of the fish.

Note: This recipe also works well with flounder and other types of fish.

Makes 6 servings.

LOBSTER THERMIDOR

2   1 1/2-pound live Maine lobsters
2   tablespoons olive oil
4   ounces lump crabmeat (picked over)
4   ounces Dungeness crabmeat (picked over)
1   shallot, sliced
3   garlic cloves, sliced
1/4   cup brandy
3/4   cup heavy cream
1   tablespoon Dijon mustard
1   ounce grated Parmesan
1   sprig fresh tarragon leaves, chopped
    Kosher salt
    Freshly ground black pepper
1   ounce Japanese panko bread crumbs

Preheat a broiler. With a sharp knife on a solid surface, put the knife through the head of the lobsters to kill them instantly. Flip them over and split lengthwise down the middle, keeping the back of the shell intact. Remove the roe and tomalley and discard. Pull the claws off and remove the tail meat from the shell; set aside.

Place the lobsters on a baking sheet and broil until bright red, about 3 to 5 minutes; set aside.

In a pot of boiling salted water, cook the lobster claws for 5 minutes. Drain and let cool at room temperature until ready to serve.

In a large skillet over medium heat add the olive oil and lobster tail meat. Cook until the meat turns white, about 2 minutes. Add the lump crabmeat and Dungeness crabmeat and stir to combine. Add the shallot and garlic and cook for 1 minute while shaking the pan to prevent burning. Remove the pan from the heat and add the brandy (the alcohol will ignite, so be careful) and return the pan to medium heat. Add the heavy cream and Dijon mustard and cook until reduced by half. Add the Parmesan and fold it in to melt. Add the chopped tarragon and season with salt and pepper.

Stuff the lobster and crab mixture into the lobster shells and sprinkle the top with the bread crumbs. Broil until browned, about 4 to 5 minutes. Reheat the claws for just 1 minute in hot water and serve with the stuffed lobsters.

Makes 2 servings.

SHRIMP TEQUILA

2   pounds extra-large (16-20) Gulf shrimp
    Salt and fresh ground pepper
1/2   cup olive oil
2   serrano peppers, sliced
1/4   cup chopped scallions
1/4   cup lime juice
2   medium garlic cloves, minced
1   orange bell pepper, diced
1/2   cup tequila
3   Roma tomatoes, seeded and diced
1   tablespoon chopped cilantro
1/4   stick butter
1   avocado, peeled, pitted, and diced

Season the shrimp with salt and fresh ground pepper. In a sauté pan over high heat add the olive oil. Add the shrimp, serrano peppers, scallions, lime juice, garlic, bell pepper, and tequila in order, stirring or flipping the pan constantly. After adding the tequila ignite the ingredients (if using an electric stove you will need to use a match). Add the tomatoes and cilantro. Turn off the heat, and stir in the butter. Top with the avocado.

Note: This is a fast-paced recipe meant to be cooked in approximately 5 minutes.

Makes 4 servings.

Southeast
BOBWHITE AND BONEFISH

The Marquesa Hotel
Pine Hill Plantation
Wynfield Plantation

THE MARQUESA HOTEL

Key West, Florida

Ernest Hemingway called Key West home, as did Tennessee Williams. It was here that Hemingway was introduced to big game fishing and the lifestyle that led to so many of his greatest stories, and it was here that Williams wrote the first draft of *A Streetcar Named Desire*. Key West is so conducive to creativity that it has spawned some of America's greatest literature and legend. Can there be a place as romantic as Key West?

Many of the original immigrants to Key West were Bahamians, the sons and daughters of British loyalists who fled to the Bahamas after the American Revolution. They called themselves "Conches" and made their fortunes through the salvaging of wrecks, smuggling, and other occupations of opportunity. It is a culture that has always been on the edge, situated on the southernmost point of the United States in a turquoise environment of such beauty as to banish all stress upon arrival.

In the heart of this marvelous and sultry culture is the Marquesa Hotel, sitting one block from Duval Street. A renovation of some of the nineteenth-century "conch" houses, stores, and even a convent, the Marquesa Hotel and the world famous Café Marquesa offer the quintessential Keys experience and have been rated by *Travel and Leisure* as one of the top ten hotels in the Untied States. Zagat survey rated the Café Marquesa as one of the top 100 hotel restaurants in the United States as well.

For the angler, this is paradise, albeit a challenging one. There can be no more beautiful experience than fishing a white sand flat in a turquoise sea, looking for bonefish, tarpon, and permit. To catch them, one must see them, and with the help of experienced guides, anglers find themselves casting to the greatest collection of gamefish, renowned for sheer speed and power. After a day on the flat here is my description:

The brilliant silver of the bonefish perfectly reflects the hues and tones that surround it. At best you learn to see apparitions. The practiced eye eventually begins to discern the fish as it moves slowly in its quest, often appearing as if suddenly revealed by the hand of a magician. Those startling moments happen often and add to the mystery of this remarkable fish. Scanning the bottom you are all too aware that you are looking at a fish and not seeing it. Perhaps the real joy of this pursuit is the never-ending surprise as the sun, the sand, the eye, and the mind suddenly conspire to give you a glimpse of the ghost.

The beauty of it all is that the most difficult of fish to see must be seen to be caught. When all is right, the bone is spotted at distance. The cast is laid in front, presenting the tiny, sparkling pseudo-crustacean in position to be pulled away as if escaping. When it settles to the bottom, a strip of the line puffs the fly across the sand. If the gods are kind, the fish suddenly darts to the fly and, tipping downward, inhales it. A long and gentle strip ensures the hook set and this silver rocket rips across the flat in pursuit of freedom—all unfolding in a blue, crystalline theater.

Hemingway, endless flats to hunt elusive fish, sultry nights, and legends of the sea—romantic? One would think.

COCONUT CRUSTED MAHI MAHI

This recipe is easier to prepare if you do some prep work ahead of time. Soak the rice noodles in hot water for 30 minutes. Prepare both sauces and set them aside. Prepare the crust and set it aside. Chop the vegetables for the stir-fry. Proceed to stir-frying the vegetables and broiling the mahi mahi.

Stir-fry Sauce
- 1 shallot, minced
- 2 teaspoons minced garlic
- 2 teaspoons minced ginger
- 1 stalk lemongrass, chopped
- 1 teaspoon sesame oil
- 1/2 cup sake
- 1 quart vegetable stock
- 2 teaspoons yellow miso paste
- 1 cup rice wine vinegar
- 1 cup soy sauce
- 1 teaspoon arrowroot dissolved in 2 teaspoons water
- 1/2 8-ounce jar hoisin sauce

Mango-Miso Sauce
- 1 shallot, minced
- 1/4 cup grated fresh ginger
- 1/4 cup yellow miso paste
- 2 teaspoons plus 1/4 cup sesame oil
- 1/2 cup sake
- 1 quart mango purée
- 1/2 cup orange juice
- 1 cup water
- 1/4 cup olive oil

Ginger Almond Coconut Crust
- 1/2 pound unsalted butter, softened
- 1/2 cup sliced almonds
- 1/2 cup unsweetened coconut
- 1/4 bunch basil leaves, thinly sliced
- 1/2 teaspoon powdered ginger
- 1 cup panko bread crumbs

Stir-fry Vegetables
- 1/4 head red cabbage, shredded
- 1/2 head napa cabbage, shredded
- 1/2 bok choy, thinly sliced on the bias
- 1 carrot, julienned
- 1 small daikon, julienned
- 3 celery stalks, thinly sliced on the bias
  Vegetable oil
- 1 pound rice noodles, soaked and drained

Mahi Mahi
- 4 6-ounce pieces mahi mahi
  Vegetable oil

For the stir-fry sauce, in a large pan sauté the shallot, garlic, ginger, and lemongrass in the sesame oil until opaque, about 3 minutes. Deglaze the pan with the sake and reduce by half. Add the stock, miso, and vinegar. Bring to a boil. Add the arrowroot mixture and hoisin sauce. Cook until slightly thickened. Let cool.

For the mango-miso sauce, combine the shallot, ginger, miso, 2 teaspoons of the sesame oil, the sake, mango purée, orange juice, and water in a food processor and purée until smooth. Drizzle in the olive oil and the remaining 1/4 cup sesame oil. Refrigerate in a squeeze bottle or container. Set aside.

For the crust, in a mixer using a paddle attachment, combine the butter, almonds, coconut, basil, ginger, and bread crumbs. Leave at room temperature.

For the stir-fry vegetables, in a large pan sauté the red cabbage, napa cabbage, bok choy, carrot, daikon, and celery for 3 minutes in vegetable oil over high heat. Add the stir-fry sauce as the vegetables begin to cook down. Coat the vegetables with the sauce, but do not saturate. Place the vegetables on a serving plate. In the pan used to cook the vegetables, add the rice noodles and toss for 1 minute to warm them. Add the noodles to the plate next to the vegetables.

For the mahi mahi, preheat the oven to 350°. Sear the fish in a sauté pan with vegetable oil. Place the fish on a baking sheet and cook in the oven until just opaque in the center, about 5 to 7 minutes. Remove the fish from the oven. Turn the oven to broil and pat the prepared crust onto the fish. Broil until the crust is crisp.

To serve, place the fish on top of the stir-fry vegetables, and spoon the mango-miso sauce over the fish.

Makes 4 servings.

CONCH AND BLUE CRAB CAKES

Cucumber Jicama Slaw

1/2 cup julienned jicama

1/2 cup julienned English cucumber

1/2 cup julienned carrots

1/2 poblano chile, finely diced

1/2 red bell pepper, finely diced

2 scallions, sliced

1/4 bunch cilantro, chopped

1/2 cup rice wine vinegar

1 teaspoon salt

1/2 teaspoon ground white pepper

1 teaspoon toasted black sesame seeds

1 teaspoon toasted white sesame seeds

Creole Tartar Sauce

1/2 red onion, chopped

1 celery stalk, chopped

1/4 red bell pepper, chopped

1/2 yellow bell pepper, chopped

1/2 jalapeño pepper, chopped

2 teaspoons capers

1 teaspoon Creole seasoning

1/2 teaspoon chili powder

1/4 teaspoon cayenne pepper

1 cup mayonnaise

1/2 cup sour cream

1 teaspoon Matouk's sauce (or similar mustard-based sauce)

1/4 bunch cilantro leaves

1/4 cup key lime juice

Salt and pepper to taste

Conch and Blue Crab Cakes

1/2 small poblano chile, diced

1/2 small red bell pepper, diced

1/2 small yellow bell pepper, diced

1/2 cup finely diced red onion

3 scallions, sliced

1/4 bunch basil, julienned

1 teaspoon olive oil

2 extra-large eggs

1/2 pound cooked ground conch

1/2 pound crabmeat

1/4 cup mayonnaise

1/8 cup pancake mix

1/2 cup panko bread crumbs

1 teaspoon chili powder

2 teaspoons Old Bay seasoning

Salt

White pepper

Shredded phyllo dough as needed

2 teaspoons canola oil

For the slaw, toss the jicama, cucumber, carrots, poblano chile, bell pepper, scallions, cilantro, vinegar, salt, white pepper, and sesame seeds together. Adjust the seasoning as desired. Set aside.

For the tartar sauce, in a blender or food processor combine the onion, celery, bell peppers, jalapeño pepper, capers, Creole seasoning, chili powder, cayenne pepper, mayonnaise, sour cream, Matouk's sauce, cilantro, key lime juice, and salt and pepper to taste. Blend until all the vegetables are finely minced. Set aside.

For the crab cakes, sauté the poblano chile, bell peppers, onion, scallions, and basil in a medium pan in the olive oil until opaque. Chill.

Lightly beat the eggs in a small bowl. Place the sautéed vegetables, the conch, and the crabmeat in a large mixing bowl. Gently fold in the mayonnaise, pancake mix, bread crumbs, chili powder, Old Bay

seasoning, salt, and white pepper. Let chill in the refrigerator for 1 hour.

Form the mixture into 4 round cakes (a mold will make it easier). Place 1 teaspoon of shredded phyllo in the bottom of each mold. Fill the mold with the crab mixture and top with 1 teaspoon of shredded phyllo.

Preheat the oven to 350°. Heat a heavy-bottomed sauté pan over medium-high heat. Add the canola oil. When the oil is slightly smoking, add the cakes and brown on each side. Place the cakes on a baking sheet and bake for 8 to 10 minutes. Turn the cakes over and cook an additional 5 to 8 minutes.

Serve the conch and blue crab cakes with the Cucumber Jicama Slaw and the Creole Tartar Sauce.

Makes 4 servings.

KEY LIME NAPOLEON

Prepare the key lime curd, fruit mixture, and raspberry sauce before baking the phyllo crackers.

Key Lime Curd

9   eggs

2   cups sugar

2   cups key lime juice

1   cup (2 sticks) butter, cubed

2   cups heavy cream, whipped

1   tablespoon confectioner's sugar

1/2 teaspoon pure vanilla extract

Fruit Mixture

1   mango, peeled and diced

1   papaya, peeled, seeded, and diced

1/2 golden pineapple, peeled and diced

1/2 pint blackberries

1/4 cup white wine

1   tablespoon sugar

1/2 pint raspberries for garnish

Raspberry Sauce

1   container frozen raspberries with syrup, thawed

Phyllo Crackers

4   sheets phyllo dough, thawed

1/2 cup clarified butter

3/4 cup sugar

1/2 cup finely chopped macadamia nuts

For the curd, whisk the eggs with the sugar and lime juice in a bowl.

In a double boiler combine the egg mixture and the butter and stir with a wooden spoon or rubber spatula over moderate heat. Be careful to not beat air into the mixture. Cook until thickened and then chill in the refrigerator.

Fold 1 cup of the whipped cream into the chilled curd; return to the refrigerator. Flavor the remaining whipped cream with the confectioner's sugar and vanilla. Refrigerate the whipped cream until you are ready to assemble the Napoleon.

For the fruit mixture, in a large bowl toss the mango, papaya, pineapple, and blackberries with wine and sugar. Set aside.

For the raspberry sauce, over low heat in a small saucepan reduce the raspberries by about half. Let cool slightly and blend in a blender. Strain through a fine strainer to remove the seeds and chill.

Note: Prepared raspberry sauce may be used.

For the phyllo crackers, preheat the oven to 350°. Unfold the thawed phyllo dough and place between two napkins; keep the dough covered until needed, removing one piece at a time. Line a sheet pan with parchment or wax paper, and place 1 sheet of phyllo dough on the pan. Brush it thoroughly with the clarified butter.

Sprinkle 1/4 cup sugar and the nuts evenly over the dough. Repeat with the remaining phyllo, ending with a phyllo layer.

Cut the dough with a pizza wheel in half horizontally and then lengthwise into 3 equal strips. Cut each piece into triangles.

Place a piece of parchment paper on top of the dough. Place another sheet pan on top of the parchment and bake for 10 to 12 minutes, until golden brown. The phyllo can burn quickly, so watch it carefully to prevent burning.

To serve, chill 4 plates, preferably white. Drizzle the raspberry sauce on each plate toward the edges (a squirt bottle makes this job easier). Place 3 dollops of the whipped cream toward the center of each plate. Place 1 cracker on each plate, balanced on the whipped cream. Place 1 dollop of the curd mixture on each cracker and top with the fruit mixture. Place another cracker in the curd mixture and fruit so it stands upright. Dust with confectioner's sugar, and garnish with fresh raspberries.

Makes 4 servings.

PINE HILL PLANTATION

Donalsonville, Georgia

T radition is taken seriously in plantation quail hunting in the deep south. Perhaps it is because tradition emanates more easily from the leisure pursuits of the wealthy than from the necessary pursuits of the yeoman. But nowhere have traditions evolved and been romanticized more than on the southern quail plantations.

There is a proper way to hunt bobwhite quail, and an etiquette born of the need for safety, combined with the gentility of southern manners. One of the hallmarks of a true plantation hunt is the mule-drawn quail wagon, and at Pine Hill Plantation this experience, usually found only on the great private plantations of the coastal plain, is nurtured to the point where the visitor is no longer a visitor, but for a moment, the owner of the plantation.

The mule is a beautiful creature with the hardiness of the donkey and the courage of the horse. A matched pair of mules is a magnificent example of harmony and efficiency, and at Pine Hill, "Jim Bob" and "John Boy" pull the quail wagon together. In a traditional quail hunt, the hunters are mounted. The dogs are put out and immediately begin to range out front. The hunt master is the lead rider, followed by the mounted hunters and then the quail wagon carrying the other pointers, refreshments, and supplies for the day's hunt. When the pointers lock up on a covey of quail, the hunt master raises his hat, the hunters dismount, unsheathe their guns, and move forward to honor the point. The covey flushes in a whirring explosion, and the report of fine shotguns signals either success or failure. To the southern quail hunter, the sight of this train moving through the open fields and pine forests is the most sacred of experiences.

Pine Hill is in the southwest corner of Georgia near the point where the Alabama/Georgia line intersects the Florida border. It is the center of bobwhite quail habitat. The two houses on the plantation, Pine Hill Manor and Quail Covey Lodge, are designed as private plantation homes into which the visitor steps as if it were his own. Amenities include a graciously-appointed

master suite, a cigar/gun room, a private dining room, a porch overlooking the private lake, a great room with fireplace, and guest rooms with private bathrooms. These two houses rival many of the plantation homes on private estates.

To partake in this experience, one needs either an invitation from one of the owners of the South's great private plantations or to visit Pine Hill Plantation.

PINE HILL PLANTATION'S STUFFED QUAIL

Stuffing

1   pound sausage
1   large onion, chopped
3   celery stalks, chopped
1   8-ounce bag corn bread stuffing (or 2 1/2 cups crumbled corn bread)
2 1/2 cups bread crumbs
2   8-ounce cans chicken broth
1/2 cup melted butter
1   teaspoon salt
1/2 teaspoon pepper
1/2 teaspoon sage
1   egg

Quail

12   quail
12   bacon strips

For the stuffing, in a skillet brown the sausage with the onion and celery; drain. In a large bowl toss the sausage mixture with the stuffing, bread crumbs, chicken broth, butter, salt, pepper, sage, and egg.

For the quail, clean the quail. Overstuff each quail with the stuffing. Tightly wrap each quail with a strip of bacon (stretching the bacon so that it stays in place without use of toothpicks). The bacon will hold the stuffing firmly in the quail.

Preheat the grill to 350°. Grill the birds indirectly over mesquite (or on the top rack of a gas grill using liberal amounts of water-soaked mesquite chips or chunks) for approximately 20 to 30 minutes until a beautiful golden brown.

Makes 12 servings.

GRILLED MARINATED BEEF TENDERLOIN

1   20-ounce can crushed pineapple, undrained
1   15-ounce bottle teriyaki sauce
1   16-ounce jar maraschino cherries, undrained
3   garlic cloves, crushed
1/4 cup vinegar
1   4- to 6-pound beef tenderloin

In a large, shallow dish combine the pineapple with juice, teriyaki sauce, cherries with juice, garlic, and vinegar.

Remove the silver skin from the beef tenderloin. Submerge the tenderloin in the marinade and refrigerate for 8 hours or more.

Preheat the gas grill to 450°. Cook the tenderloin on the top rack for 5 minutes per pound (to sear in flavor), watching closely so that fat drippings do not flame up. Reduce the heat to 200° for 15 minutes per pound or until the center is 125° (10° shy of medium rare). Remove from the grill and allow to rest as cooking will continue. Slice and serve.

Note: Can also be cooked in the oven as follows: Preheat the oven to 450°. Cook on the top rack for 5 minutes per pound (to sear in flavor). Use the vent hood to ventilate the kitchen as the tenderloin will smoke when cooking at 450°. Reduce the heat to 200° for 15 minutes per pound or until the center is 125° (10° shy of medium rare). Remove from oven and allow to rest as cooking will continue. Slice and serve.

Makes 8 to 12 servings.

ROSALYNN CARTER'S PEANUT BUTTER PIE

1/2 cup sugar

1/4 cup cornstarch

2   cups milk

3   eggs, separated

1   tablespoon butter

1   teaspoon vanilla extract

1   cup confectioner's sugar

1 1/2 cups peanut butter

1   pre-baked 9-inch piecrust

4   teaspoon sugar

Preheat the oven to 325°. In a small saucepan mix the sugar and cornstarch together. Add the milk and egg yolks. Cook over low heat, stirring constantly until thick. Stir in the butter and vanilla. Set aside.

In a medium bowl mix the confectioner's sugar and peanut butter and spread two-thirds of it in the bottom of the piecrust.

In a mixing bowl beat the egg whites until foamy. Gradually add the sugar until stiff peaks form.

Pour the filling on top of the peanut butter layer.

Spread the meringue over the filling. Sprinkle the remaining peanut butter mixture on top of the meringue. Bake for 8 to 15 minutes or until the meringue is light brown.

Makes 8 servings.

CHOCOLATE PECAN PIE

1   cup chopped Georgia pecans

1   9-inch piecrust

2   eggs, slightly beaten

1   cup light Karo syrup (or similar corn syrup)

1/4 cup sugar

2   tablespoons flour

1/4 teaspoon salt

1   teaspoon vanilla extract

1   cup semisweet chocolate chips

Preheat the oven to 375°. Spread the pecans over the piecrust. In a bowl mix the eggs, corn syrup, sugar, flour, salt, vanilla, and chocolate chips. Pour over the pecans and bake for 40 to 50 minutes or until set.

Makes one 9-inch pie.

WYNFIELD PLANTATION

Albany, Georgia

The word *plantation* conjures for the sporting gentry a very specific vision of great pointing dogs, live oaks festooned with Spanish moss, pine forests, and the wonderful bobwhite quail. Of all hunting experiences, the plantation quail hunt is perhaps the most civilized, the one most imbued with tradition. Wynfield Plantation was created for no other reason than to bring that experience home to its patrons.

South of Albany, Georgia, is the heart of plantation quail country. Here where the rolling piedmont ends and the coastal plain begins, the quail hunting tradition is deeply ingrained in the fabric and culture of the region. At a certain moment traveling south, the roads lose their curve and the ground settles flat. Live oaks appear, dripping moss, and the soil turns from red clay to sand. Old houses still reside on pier foundations, surrounded by pecan orchards that offer shade in the heat of summer and provide the basis for some of the South's greatest delicacies. When you walk this country, gun in hand, the low briars pulling at your legs, the dogs quartering in front, there is no doubt of your quarry. There is perhaps no more remarkable moment in hunting than the explosion of a quail covey in front of a rigid brace of dogs. The birds streak into the pines like bottle rockets, followed by often futile shots. Here, quickness and accuracy are virtues.

Bill Bowles grew up in this tradition, working at plantations and learning from the old managers who spent their lives training dogs and horses, managing habitat, and maintaining the quail hunting traditions. When the opportunity arose he created Wynfield. The main lodge houses the great room, the dining room, the pro shop, and a large veranda where guests gather after dinner to swap tales of shots missed and made. The siren call of the bobwhite quail rides the warm wind through the pines as guests drift back to the three beautifully appointed cabins.

Wynfield cuisine is created in the deepest traditions of southern cooking. The staples are simple, since traditional southern cooking takes its roots from what is most available: grits, collards, field peas and beans, turnip greens, biscuits, and with luck the bobwhite quail. Over the years this simple fare has become synonymous with the graceful lifestyle that is the plantation South.

MAPLE ROASTED QUAIL

2   tablespoons butter
2   tablespoons maple syrup
    Pinch of garlic powder
    Salt and pepper to taste
4   quail, cleaned

Melt the butter in a skillet over medium-high heat. Add the maple syrup, garlic powder, and salt and pepper. Reduce the heat to simmer.

Preheat the oven to 375°. Using string or toothpicks, tie the quail legs together. Brush the quail with half the maple syrup mixture and place on a wire rack in a baking tray. Place in the oven and roast for 10 minutes. Remove the quail from the oven and baste with the remaining maple butter. Return to the oven and continue to roast until fully cooked (10 to 15 minutes longer) and golden brown, basting every 5 minutes. Remove from the oven and serve on the Sweet Potato Polenta (see recipe on opposite page) and garnish with the Mission Fig and Caramelized Shallot Compote (see following recipe).

Makes 4 servings

MISSION FIG AND CARAMELIZED SHALLOT COMPOTE

2   tablespoons butter
1/4 cup chopped garlic
1/2 cup peeled and quartered shallots
1/2 cup halved dried mission figs
1   cup chicken stock
1/2 cup apple cider
1   teaspoon fresh chopped thyme
1   tablespoon freshly chopped parsley
    Salt and pepper to taste

Melt the butter in a skillet over medium-high heat. Sauté the garlic and shallots in the butter until evenly browned. Add the figs, chicken stock, and apple cider. Bring to a boil, then reduce to a simmer. Simmer, uncovered, until the liquid reduces by two-thirds and begins to thicken. Add thyme, parsley, and salt and pepper. Keep warm and serve with the quail. Can be made a day ahead and stored in the refrigerator and warmed before serving.

Makes 4 servings.

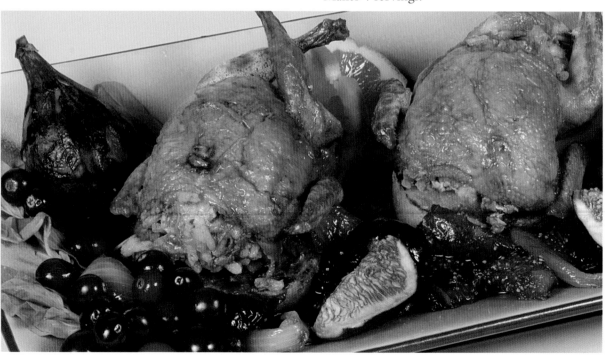

SWEET POTATO POLENTA

4 tablespoons butter
2 shallots, minced
1 garlic clove, minced
2 cups chicken stock
1 cup cornmeal
2 egg yolks
2 cups cooked and mashed sweet potato
   Pinch of nutmeg
   Pinch of allspice
   Salt and pepper to taste
3 tablespoons butter, melted

Melt the butter in a skillet over medium–high heat. Sauté the shallots and garlic in the butter until the shallots become translucent. Add the chicken stock and bring to a boil. Add the cornmeal in a steady stream while stirring. Reduce the heat to low and allow the mixture to cook for about 10 minutes, stirring often. Remove from heat.

Combine the egg yolks with the sweet potatoes and then add into the cornmeal mixture. Mix well (use an electric mixer or mix with a wooden spoon). Add the nutmeg, allspice, and salt and pepper and mix well.

Preheat the oven to 350°. Grease a baking sheet with cooking spray or shortening. Dust the greased baking sheet with flour, shaking off any excess. Turn out the cornmeal potato mixture onto the baking sheet. With a rolling pin, roll the mixture to 3/4-inch thickness. Bake for 20 to 30 minutes, or until a wooden toothpick inserted into the center of the pan comes out clean (145°). Remove from the oven and allow to cool thoroughly. Refrigerate until firm.

Preheat the oven to 350°. Remove the Polenta from the refrigerator and portion with a 3-inch biscuit cutter. Brush the melted butter on top of each portion and bake until the edges begin to brown. Top with quail and serve with fig compote.

Makes 4 servings.

RUSTIC CHEDDAR CHEESE AND SAGE BISCUITS

2 1/2 cups all-purpose flour
1 teaspoon salt
2 tablespoons baking powder
1 tablespoon chopped fresh sage
1 teaspoon course ground black pepper
1 1/4 cups buttermilk
1/2 cup shredded cheddar cheese

In a medium bowl combine the flour, salt, baking powder, sage, and pepper. Add the buttermilk and mix until ingredients are just combined. Add the cheddar cheese and mix again until just combined. Remove from the bowl and form into one ball of dough. Wrap with plastic wrap and refrigerate for 1 hour.

Preheat the oven to 375°.

On a well–floured surface roll the biscuit dough to a thickness of 1 inch. Using a 2 1/2-inch round cookie cutter, cut the biscuits and place them on a greased cookie sheet spaced 2 inches apart.

Brush the biscuits with a light coating of buttermilk, then sprinkle with flour for a rustic appearance. Allow the biscuits to come to room temperature before baking. Place them in the oven for 20 to 30 minutes, or until lightly browned. Best served while still warm.

Note: you can reform the scrap dough to cut additional biscuits.

Makes 8 to 10 biscuits.

ZINFANDEL PORT WINE POACHED PEARS

1 1/2 cups Zinfandel wine

1 cup Port wine

1 cup water

1 cup sugar

1 teaspoon whole Szechwan peppercorns

6 whole allspice berries

4 Bosc pears, peeled and cored

In a medium saucepan combine the Zinfandel wine, Port, water, sugar, peppercorns, and berries. Bring the mixture to a boil. Reduce the heat to a simmer and cook uncovered for 5 minutes.

Add the pears and continue to simmer for an additional 20 to 25 minutes, or until the pears are cooked yet remain slightly firm. While boiling, turn the pears often so that they color evenly. Remove the pears from the wine syrup and place on a rack to cool.

Strain and reserve the wine syrup to be used in Wine-Scented Chocolate Ganache recipe that follows.

Makes 4 servings.

WINE-SCENTED CHOCOLATE GANACHE

1 cup semisweet chocolate chips

1/2 cup heavy cream

2 tablespoons Zinfandel wine

1 cup strained wine syrup (see previous recipe)

4 sprigs fresh mint for garnish

Place the chocolate chips in a small bowl. Set the bowl over a warm water bath, just barely simmering at 125°, and gently heat until the chocolate is just melted. In a separate small bowl combine the cream and wine, and warm to 125°. Combine with the melted chocolate and mix well. Allow the mixture to cool.

When the ganache has partially solidified, use it to fill the core hole in the cooked pears. Chill in the refrigerator for at least one hour.

Pool a ladle of the strained wine syrup (reserved from previous recipe) in the center of a plate and place a chilled pear in the syrup. Allow the pear and ganache to come to room temperature before serving. Pears may also be served slightly warm. Garnish with a sprig of fresh mint.

Makes 4 servings.

West
BIG COUNTRY

The Alisal Guest Ranch and Golf Resort
Highland Hills Ranch
Oasis Springs Lodge
Vermejo Park Ranch

THE ALISAL GUEST RANCH AND GOLF RESORT

Solvang, California

The name *Alisal* means "sycamore grove" in Spanish. This is old California, the California of farmers and ranchers, the California that people struggled westward in wagon trains to settle. Alisal, an important piece of California history, is in the spectacular Santa Ynez Valley just over the mountains from Santa Barbara. Now home to a number of wineries, the Santa Ynez has long been an agricultural valley, and the residents today work very hard to defend it and keep it that way.

In 1843, thirty-nine years after the Spanish padres established Mission Santa Inés, Conquistador Raimundo Carrillo received the 13,500-acre Rancho Nojoqui land grant as payment for his services to the Mexican government. Carrillo immediately began raising cattle, a tradition that continues at Alisal today.

Subsequent owners the Pierce family bred harness racing's legendary trotter Lou Dillon. Horse and cattle breeder Charles Perkins bought the property in 1927 and raised Kentucky Derby winner Flying Ebony.

Once opened as a guest ranch in 1946, Alisal became a retreat for some of Hollywood's best-known citizens such as Groucho Marx and Gregory Peck. Clark Gable was married to Lady Sylvia Ashley here. But it is the fact Alisal has not changed that much and continues to be a working cattle ranch and farm that attracts many. There are no phones or television in the rooms, and cell phone coverage is non-existent. It is quite simply a place to retreat from a far too fast-paced world and be refreshed in old California.

The bungalows and accommodations are classic California ranch style, low slung and tucked in the shade of the oaks to keep them cool.

As guests would expect from a California ranch, there are horses, tennis, golf, and world-class bass fishing in a 100-acre spring fed lake that is one of the best bass lakes in California. With all natural spawn and wild fish that are catch-and-release only, the quality of the fishery only gets better with each passing year. Depending on the time of day, anglers can fish for bass on top, which to the dedicated bass angler is the epitome of largemouth bass fishing. Guides in modern bass boats put angling guests right on top of the best fishing holes in the lake.

Modern California has a mystique that beckons some and repels others. It is too big, too fast, too expensive, and sooner or later it's going to fall into the ocean. But there is a reason that over the years, people flocked to California. There was something magical about the climate, there was great hope; California was the promised land. It was Shangri-La. Nothing has changed at Alisal. Shangri-La still exists here, and old California still beckons.

CHICKEN AND SHRIMP FRICASSEE

Alisal Creole Seasoning

2 1/2	tablespoons paprika
2	tablespoons salt
2	tablespoons garlic powder
1	tablespoon freshly ground black pepper
1	tablespoon onion powder
1	tablespoon cayenne pepper
1	tablespoon dried oregano
1	tablespoon dried thyme

Fricassee

1/2	pound skinned, boned chicken breasts, cut into strips
1	tablespoon Alisal Creole Seasoning (see recipe)
1/4	cup olive oil
1	onion, cut in half vertically and sliced
1	tablespoon minced garlic
1/2	pound peeled and deveined jumbo shrimp
1/2	cup peeled, seeded, and chopped Italian plum tomatoes
2	tablespoons chopped fresh basil
2	tablespoons chopped fresh sage
1/2	cup chicken stock
1/2	teaspoon salt
	Pinch of ground black pepper

For the seasoning, combine the paprika, salt, garlic powder, black pepper, onion powder, cayenne pepper, oregano, and thyme thoroughly in a bowl. This makes 2/3 cup, 1 tablespoon of which you will use for this recipe. The remaining seasoning can be stored for three months in an airtight container away from light.

For the fricassee, in a bowl toss the chicken strips with 1 tablespoon of the Creole seasoning.

In a pan, sauté the chicken strips in the olive oil over medium heat until golden brown, about 4 minutes. Add the onion, garlic, shrimp, tomatoes, basil, and sage and sauté for 3 minutes. Pour in the chicken broth. Cover and simmer until the chicken is cooked through, about 2 minutes. Season with salt and pepper.

Remove the pan from the heat and keep warm. Serve the fricassee over a bed of rice or pasta.

Makes 4 servings.

BRAISED OSSO BUCCO WITH MERLOT WINE AND ORANGE ZEST

- 6   veal shanks
       Flour for dredging
- 1/2 cup (or more) olive oil
- 1   medium onion, diced
- 2   small carrots, diced
- 1   celery stalk, diced
- 1   bay leaf
- 3   cups Merlot
- 1 1/2 cups diced Roma tomatoes
- 1   teaspoon tomato paste
- 2   garlic cloves, minced
- 1 1/2 tablespoons chopped fresh parsley
- 1   tablespoon orange zest
       Salt and fresh ground pepper to taste

Dredge the veal shanks in flour and brown in a large sauté pan with some of the olive oil. Remove the shanks to a warm tray.

Add additional olive oil to the pan and sauté the onion, carrots, celery, and bay leaf. Cook for 5 minutes and add the wine. Simmer until most of the wine has evaporated from the pan.

Add the veal shanks to the pan with the tomatoes and tomato paste. Cover and simmer for 1 1/2 hours or until tender.

Remove the shanks from the pan and strain the sauce. Add the garlic, parsley, and orange zest to the sauce, and season with salt and pepper.

To serve, place the veal shanks on a platter and spoon the sauce over the meat.

Makes 6 servings.

WILD RICE AND SMOKED SCALLOP CHOWDER

1   pound onions, chopped
8   ounces carrots, chopped
8   ounces celery, chopped
1   tablespoon chopped garlic
2   bay leaves
1   cup flour
2   quarts canned clam juice
1   pound red potatoes, chopped
2 1/2 quarts milk
1   cup heavy cream
2   pounds smoked bay scallops
6   cups cooked wild rice
   Salt and pepper to taste
   Tabasco sauce to taste
   Worcestershire sauce to taste

In a heavy pot sauté the onions, carrots, celery, garlic, and bay leaves until transparent, about 5 minutes.

Add the flour and cook to make a blond roux. Add the clam juice slowly and work it into the roux to dissolve any lumps that might form.

Simmer for 20 minutes. Add the potatoes, milk, and cream and cook for 10 minutes. Add the smoked scallops and cooked wild rice.

Adjust the seasoning to taste with salt, pepper, Tabasco, and Worcestershire sauce.

Makes 1 gallon.

GODIVA CHOCOLATE CHEESECAKE

Crust

1 1/2 cups graham cracker crumbs
1/2 cup (1 stick) melted butter
1/4 cup sugar

Filling

2   cups cream cheese, softened
2   cups sugar
6   eggs
1/2 cup cream
2   teaspoons vanilla extract
2/3 cup cocoa powder
1/3 cup Godiva chocolate liqueur

Topping

3   cups sour cream
1   cup confectioner's sugar
1   tablespoon vanilla extract
3   tablespoons cocoa powder
1   tablespoon Godiva chocolate liqueur

For the crust, coat a 12-inch pie pan with cooking spray. Mix the graham cracker crumbs, melted butter, and sugar in a food processor until moist and soft. Press the crust mixture into the prepared pan.

For the filling, preheat the oven to 325°. In a large bowl, beat the cream cheese and sugar together. Add the eggs one at a time. Add the cream and vanilla. Mix until blended. Add the cocoa powder and chocolate liqueur. Pour the filling into the crust. Bake for 40 to 45 minutes. Let the cheesecake stand for 5 minutes.

For the topping, combine the sour cream, confectioner's sugar, vanilla, cocoa powder, and liqueur in a bowl and whisk together until well blended. Spread the topping over the cooled cheesecake before serving.

Makes 8 servings.

HIGHLAND HILLS RANCH
Condon, Oregon

Many experts say that the best hunting preserve in the country is Highland Hills Ranch. That's a pretty strong claim, but it is not a claim that Highland Hills makes itself. It is a claim made by many who have hunted all over the country. What better testimonial than from experienced hunters? What is the reason? Habitat.

Highland Hills is a 3,000-acre working farm in north central Oregon. But whereas most farmers utilize every square inch of tillable land to maximize profits, Highland Hills discovered it could make a better living by farming wild birds. The farming here is done with agricultural practices that offer food and shelter for wildlife, edge cover, water, and grains.

Gary Lewis, an outdoor writer from Oregon, describes it this way:

As we drove onto the ranch, I was impressed with the habitat. Corn and barley stood unharvested. Milo and sunflowers grew along the creek. Native grasses stood thick and tall. Best sign of all, pheasants ran out of the grass and up the road in front of us. A covey of quail flushed as we drew near.

The Macnabs harvest very little of the crops on their property. Corn stands seven feet high and barley reaches to your shoulder. Instead of planting in rows, the corn and milo is sewn by broadcast. Alfalfa is growing volunteer beneath the standing grains, creating tangled understory.

Wild pheasants, chukar, Hungarian partridge, and valley quail live along the creek bottoms, and up on the flats and high benches. Mule deer filter down out of the draws and onto the fields, nipping the heads of the standing grain.

Combine these practices with a beautiful 10,000-square foot log lodge, extraordinary cuisine, a world-class wine cellar with wine tastings that are evening events, and you have one of the best experiences one could hope for with a shotgun.

There are a number of opportunities for wing shooters. The bottom lands offer pheasant, quail, and chukars, while the hardiest of hunter can traverse the steep hillsides for Hungarian partridge. But what makes this so appealing is that the shooting is unlimited. Extraordinary game management allows this gunning preserve to continue to offer such quality hunting from August through March.

A new twist added recently is British-style driven pheasant shoots in which the shooters are stationary and the pheasants are flying high and fast overhead in a the classic European style. This takes a great deal of skill, and the lodge offers a full day of instruction in this type of shooting prior to the hunt. It is the crowning touch to what is hailed by many as the best in its class.

Layne Simpson, an outdoor writer and a Field Editor for *Shooting Times*, a man who has seen a lot of hunts in a lot of places, put it this way. "The only thing I could find to complain about was our stay didn't last a month."

BRAISED PHEASANT

2 tablespoons olive oil

1 large onion, sliced

6 pheasant breasts

5 tablespoons all-purpose flour

1 teaspoon course salt (or sea salt)

2 tablespoons unsalted butter, divided

1 cup low-sodium chicken broth

1/4 cup dry white wine

1 teaspoon chopped fresh thyme (or 1/2 teaspoon dry)

1/2 pound sliced mushrooms

Pinch of salt

Chopped fresh parsley for garnish

Heat the oil over medium heat in a large sauté pan. Sauté the onion in the oil until soft, approximately 8 minutes. Remove the onion from the pan, and set aside.

Place the pheasant breasts in a plastic zip-top bag. Add the flour and salt and shake the bag to coat the pheasant breasts; tap off excess flour.

Melt 1 tablespoon of the butter in the same sauté pan. Add the pheasant and sauté until lightly browned (do not overcook, as it will make the meat dry and tough).

Layer the cooked onions over the top of the pheasant and add the chicken broth, wine, and thyme. Cover and simmer until the meat is tender, about 30 minutes.

In a separate skillet, melt the remaining tablespoon of butter. Add the mushrooms and sauté until soft, about 4 to 5 minutes. Add a pinch of salt. Add the mushroom mixture to the pheasant breasts after the pheasant has been cooking for 20 minutes.

Place the breasts on serving plates and garnish with parsley.

Serve with roasted vegetables and small red potatoes.

Makes 6 servings.

PHEASANT ENCHILADAS

4 to 6 pheasant breasts
   White wine or bottled salsa for simmering
2 10 1/2-ounce cans cream of chicken soup
1 pint sour cream
1 4-ounce can chopped green chiles (reserve some for garnish)
1 dozen small flour tortillas (corn tortillas may also be used)
3/4 large onion, chopped
3 to 4 cups grated Cheddar and Monterey Jack cheese
   Black olives for garnish
   Chopped green onions for garnish

In a large stockpot, simmer the pheasant breasts in white wine or salsa for 3 hours. Make sure the pheasant is very tender. Shred or chop the pheasant into small pieces.

Preheat the oven to 350°. Mix the pheasant, soup, sour cream, and most of the chiles together. Spread a thin layer of the creamed mixture over the bottom of a 12x9-inch metal pan or glass baking dish. Spread equal amounts of the creamed mixture down the middle of each tortilla, reserving some of the mixture for the top. Sprinkle with the chopped onion and cheese, reserving some of the cheese for the top. (The chopped onion may be mixed into the creamed mixture, as opposed to sprinkling it on top of the mixture.) Roll up the tortillas and place, seam side down, in the prepared pan. Pour the remaining creamed mixture over the top of the rolled tortillas and sprinkle with the remaining cheese. Bake for 25 to 30 minutes.

Garnish with black olives, green onions, and the reserved chiles. We also garnish with picco de gallo or homemade salsa.

Makes 6 to 8 servings.

OASIS SPRINGS LODGE

Paynes Creek, California

In 1915 Lassen Peak erupted, spewing lava and ash for almost 200 miles. Lassen Peak has been quiet since then, and, according to scientists, chances are it's not going to blow off any steam for about 10,000 more years. That's the good news. The better news is that nestled in the shadow of Lassen is a spectacular 4,000-acre ranch, tucked away at the end of a six-mile drive. Perched on the banks of Battle Creek, an absolutely pristine, clear tributary of the mighty Sacramento River, is Oasis Springs Lodge, an Orvis-endorsed fly-fishing lodge with six miles of private water of the south fork of this magnificent stream.

Battle Creek averages twenty feet across and tumbles down an often narrow canyon that has one pool and riffle after another, full of native rainbows. Pure spring water with a little snowmelt from neighboring volcanic peaks makes for a crystal-clear, pollution-free stream. On the private water of the ranch there are fifteen pools from the easy home pool in front of the lodge to more remote and challenging pools.

The stream is full of native trout, and steelhead and salmon making their runs to their birthplaces upstream. There are no stocked fish here, and what the angler receives from this river is an experience that hasn't changed since the volcanoes formed 10,000 years ago. It's a rugged wilderness atmosphere, full of wildlife: deer, eagles, river otters, osprey, black bears, grouse, and game birds. Little has changed in the years since it was home to Ishi and his California Indian ancestors.

Ishi, which means man—it was taboo in his culture to speak one's name—was the name given to the last member of the Yahi, the last surviving group of the Yana people of California. Ishi is believed to have been the last Native American in Northern California to have lived the bulk of his life completely outside the European American culture. He emerged from the wild near Oroville, California, in 1911, after leaving his ancestral homeland in the foothills near Lassen Peak, and was taken to the Anthropological Department at The University of California, San Francisco, where he lived the rest of his life, helping scientists reconstruct his vanished culture.

It is his land, still in the pristine state it was when his ancestors roamed the hills, that Oasis Springs resides. Constructed in 1991, the beautiful lodge boasts over 12,000 square feet of living space to suit the most discriminating of guests. One of its most striking features is the huge porch, the perfect place to spend a relaxing afternoon reading or dozing. Surrounded by trees and landscaped paths, the lodge sits mere feet from the bank of the trout-filled river and comfortably accommodates up to twenty-two people.

This is a true ecological experience. Other than the lodge, which offers extraordinary comfort, this is a place where the world remains as it was and perhaps as it should be.

SUMMER SALAD

1	head Romaine lettuce, chopped
	Watermelon and cantaloupe, cut into bite-size pieces
	Cherries
1	6-ounce container peach yogurt
1	6-ounce container orange yogurt
1/4	cup orange juice
1/4	cup raspberry walnut vinaigrette

Place the chopped Romaine on 4 chilled plates, and add the desired amounts of watermelon, cantaloupe, and strawberries.

In a bowl, stir together the yogurts, orange juice, and vinaigrette. Pour over the salad and serve.

Makes 4 servings.

ITALIAN SPECIAL

1	cup (2 sticks) butter
1	pound smoked ground ham
1	tablespoon minced garlic
1	10-ounce package frozen chopped spinach, thawed and drained
1	cup cream
	Salt and pepper
2	tablespoons vodka
8	ounces penne rigate, cooked according to package directions
	Freshly grated Parmesan

In a large pan over medium heat, melt the butter and add the ham, garlic, and spinach. Reduce the heat to low and cook until just heated. Add the cream and cook until just heated. Drizzle the vodka into the pan.

Spoon the sauce over the cooked pasta and top with freshly grated Parmesan and salt and pepper to taste.

Makes 4 servings.

BARBECUE SPARE RIBS

1   8-ounce can crushed pineapple, undrained
    Dark brown sugar
2   slabs spareribs, about 4 pounds
    Salt and pepper
    Paprika

In a saucepan over medium heat, combine the pineapple with juice with enough brown sugar to make a thick sauce. Cook until the sauce is very thick, stirring frequently. Brush the sauce onto the ribs.

Preheat the grill to low. Cut the slab of ribs into single ribs and heavily salt and pepper both sides. Sprinkle a good amount of paprika on both sides. Place on the grill and cover. Turn the ribs every 30 minutes, basting after each turn, being careful not to burn the ribs. Cook for 2 hours, or until the ribs are done.

Makes 6 servings.

VERMEJO PARK RANCH

Raton, New Mexico

Sangre de Cristo is Spanish for "blood of Christ." Running southeast from Colorado into northern New Mexico is the southernmost range of the Rockies, the Sangre de Cristo mountains. The name derives from the blood red color of the mountains at sunrise and sunset, particularly when the peaks are covered in snow. It is a magnificent range of mountains with many "fourteeners," or peaks over 14,000 feet, offering some of the most spectacular wilderness still left in the lower forty-eight states.

Vermejo Park Ranch is the largest landholding of the largest landholder in the world, Ted Turner, and encompasses over 588,000 acres of wilderness in the northern New Mexico portion of the Sangre de Cristo range. Vermejo Park is the heart of the famous two-million acre Maxwell Land Grant, which was created in 1841 and named after Lucien Maxwell, a fur trader colleague of Kit Carson. Over the years various owners acquired and managed the property, including a group of businessmen in the 1920s who turned it into a private club, with members including Douglas Fairbanks and Mary Pickford, as well as business and political titans Harvey Firestone and Herbert Hoover.

Ted Turner is committed to returning the ranch to its ecological origins through a variety of ambitious projects including the reintroduction of the prairie dog, the black-footed ferret, the American bison, and sustainable wolf populations. The ranch also has thriving populations of black bear, coyotes, and even mountain lions. Vermejo is home to one of the last bastions of the Rio Grande cutthroat trout and their habitat is actively being expanded and protected. Over sixty percent of the land is Ponderosa Pine forest and through the use of select cutting and the controlled burning of over 20,000 acres a year, Vermejo is returning this ecosystem to a state not seen since the arrival of the first Europeans.

In returning this ranch to its original ecological state, the hunting and fishing is returning as well. Twenty-one lakes and more than thirty miles of pristine streams offer anglers the opportunity to fish for big browns, rainbows, native brook trout, and the Rio Grande cutthroat in their natural environment. Hunters can pursue elk, pronghorn antelope, mule deer, turkey, and even bison. Given the vastness of the ranch, there are distinct ecosystems, from the alpine tundra of the west side, to the high prairie grasslands on the east side of the range.

Very rarely can a single landholding this large be found. Even rarer is a commitment from the owner to spend the resources necessary to bring it back to its original state and offer it to the discerning sportsman. The Vermejo Park Ranch is unquestionably a must for any sportsman who wants to experience the great southwest as it was long before the incursion of the Anglo/Europeans.

ELK CHATEAUBRIAND WITH CHILIED CRÈME

Elk tenderloin is a favorite at Vermejo Park Ranch: as an entrée chateaubriand style and especially as an appetizer with chilied crème. Try a specialty foods market selling a farm-raised venison if you can't find elk in your area. You may also substitute beef or pork tenderloin for the elk. This dish may be served as an entrée. Make the chili crème before grilling the tenderloin. Serve the tenderloin whole on a platter, and drizzle with chilied crème.

Chilied Crème

- 1/2 cup (1 stick) unsalted butter
- 1/2 cup half-and-half
- 1/4 cup ancho chili powder
- 1   teaspoon salt
- 1/2 teaspoon pepper
- 1/4 cup diced onion

Elk

- 1/4 cup olive oil
- 1   teaspoon salt
- 1   teaspoon pepper
- 2   elk tenderloins, trimmed

For the chilied crème, combine the butter and the half-and-half in a sauté pan on medium-low heat and cook until the butter has melted. Whisk in the chili powder, salt, pepper, and onion, stirring constantly. Do not bring the sauce to a boil, but allow it to simmer to absorb the chili and onion flavor. Taste and add more salt and pepper if desired. Remove from the heat.

For the elk, mix the olive oil, salt, and pepper together in a shallow dish and dredge the whole tenderloins in the mixture. Let the tenderloins stand while pre-heating the grill. Grill the tenderloins evenly to the desired internal temperature of 112° for medium rare.

Makes 8 servings.

OSSO BUCCO WITH ROSEMARY LEMON GREMOLADA

Osso bucco, or "pierced bone," is traditionally served in a large bowl, atop risotto, rice, polenta, or mashed potatoes. The broth is used as a stew in topping the veal. A gremolada (a combination of lemon rind, parsley, and rosemary) is then used to garnish the dish. The bone marrow can be eaten and should be accessible in the shank. This dish is truly a Vermejo favorite!

Osso Bucco

3	cups flour
3	tablespoons salt
2	teaspoons pepper
1	cup vegetable oil
8	veal shanks
1	bottle merlot or red cooking wine
2	onions, diced
2	cups diced carrots
2	cups whole stewed tomatoes
1/2	cup peeled garlic
12	ounces tomato paste

Gremolada

Lemon rind
Fresh parsley
Fresh rosemary sprigs

For the gremolada, thinly shave off the yellow of a lemon rind and mince. Finely chop the parsley and rosemary together and add to the lemon rind. The mixture should be half green and half yellow.

For the osso bucco, in a shallow dish combine the flour, salt, and pepper. Mix well.

Heat the oil in a large sauté pan. Dredge the veal shanks in the flour mixture and add to the oil. Brown the shanks on both sides.

In a large mixing bowl add the wine, onions, carrots, tomatoes, garlic, and tomato paste. Toss together and let stand for 10 minutes.

Preheat the oven to 270°. In a roasting pan add the wine mixture and then place each shank into the roasting pan. Cover and place in the oven for 5 to 6 hours. At this point the veal should be tender and show signs of pulling away from the bone.

Before serving uncover the dish and, using a ladle or spoon, skim any oil off the top of the cooking juices.

To serve, place the veal shanks on a plate. Spoon the broth over the meat and garnish with the gremolada. Serve with sliced grilled bread.

Makes 8 servings.

SANGRE DE CRISTO WILD RASPBERRY CHOCOLATE TART

Tart

Vegetable oil (for pan)

1   cup cocoa powder

2   cups sifted all-purpose flour

1   teaspoon baking soda

1   teaspoon baking powder

1/2 teaspoon salt

1 1/2 cups sugar

1   stick butter, softened

2   teaspoons vanilla

2   eggs

1   cup milk

Raspberry Purée

2   cups raspberries, divided

1/2 cup merlot

1/4 cup balsamic vinegar

1   cup sugar

1/2 cup water

Whipped cream

Melted chocolate

8 to 10 mint leaves for a garnish

For the tart, preheat the oven to 350°. Grease a cookie sheet with vegetable oil. In a large bowl mix together the cocoa powder, flour, baking soda, baking powder, and salt. In another large bowl, cream together the sugar and butter using a mixer. Add the vanilla and the eggs, one at a time, while still mixing. Pour the milk into the dry ingredients. Add the butter mixture into the milk and flour mixture and fold until smooth.

Pour the batter onto the prepared cookie sheet and spread thin. Bake until a toothpick inserted into the center comes out clean, about 10 to 12 minutes; let cool. Once cool and ready for plating, cut 16 circles out of the tart, using a round cup.

For the raspberry purée, in a saucepan add 1 1/2 cups of the raspberries, the wine, vinegar, sugar, and water. Simmer until the mixture reduces by half. Let the mixture cool.

Place the cooled mixture in a blender and purée until smooth. Strain through a fine mesh strainer, pushing the purée through the strainer and discarding the seeds.

To serve, ladle the raspberry purée onto 8 dessert plates. Place one tart in the center of the purée and add a spoonful of whipped cream. Add the second tart, pressing to stabilize, and drizzle with chocolate. Garnish with mint leaves and the remaining 1/2 cup raspberries.

Note: Place foil under the cookie sheet during baking in case the tart bubbles over.

Makes 8 servings.

AUTHOR ACKNOWLEDGEMENTS

We would like to thank the Orvis Company, Leigh Perkins, Perk Perkins, and Tom Rosenbauer for allowing us to do this under the Orvis brand umbrella which we value highly. We would like to thank Scott McEnaney and Tom Evenson of the Orvis Sporting Traditions division for helping us contact and work with the lodges in this endeavor.

Our sincere thanks to Thomas Nelson Publishers for believing in this project and agreeing to take it on. Thanks to Band-F Ltd. for helping create the book and f-Stop Fitzgerald and Bruce Curtis for all their work photographing and assembling the book.

In particular, we would like to thank Mie Kingsley who coordinated all of our efforts and without whom this book would have never come together.

Finally we would most like to thank the lodges for their participation and for the wonderful services they provide to all of us who love and respect the great sporting traditions of this country.

PHOTOGRAPHER ACKNOWLEDGEMENTS

We would like to thank the authors Jim Lepage and Paul Fersen for allowing us to collaborate on this project.

We wish to thank all the lodges for joining in our adventure, and their hospitality and cooperation while we asked thousands of questions trying to get the recipes right. While there are too many to thank individually, key individuals at several of the lodges include: Ben Turpin and Mike Ramos at Pocono Manor Lodge, Kay Maghan at Nemacolin, Damon Newpher and Charles Zeran at Glendorn, Carol Wightman at The Marquesa, Alexandra and Michelle Hanten at Morrisons, Lannie Johnson at Oasis Springs, Amanda Dunn at Triple Creek, and Cynthia Gose at Dos Angeles.

Thanks to Bill Pekala and Melissa DeBartolo of Nikon Professional Services, and Jon LaCorte of Nikon Sport Optics, for allowing us the use of lenses, 35mm and compact cameras, scopes, and binoculars.

Thanks to Visit Florida, the state tourism agency, especially Paul Kayemba and Cassie Henderson. For great help photographing fly fishing in Florida, thanks to Capt. Mark Ward of Everglades Angler, Capt. Bruce Hitchcock in Chokoloskee, FL, Capt. Dan Malzone, Capt. Ralph Allen, and Capt. Les Hill.

While shooting in Florida, generous accommodations were granted by Best Western Waterfront, Fishermen's Village, Harbor Pointe Condominium Resort, and Palm Island Resort. Additional accommodations were provided by Rob DeCastro and Jane Watkins, of the Lemon Tree Inn, Naples; Sasha Hlozek at the famous Cheeca Lodge in Islamorada; the Spring Hill Suites in Tampa; the Innisbrook Resort & Golf Club in Palm Harbor; and Cathleen Casper at Key West's magnificent Casa Marina Resort.

There are many local and state tourism agencies that were extremely helpful in creating this book: Bill AuCoin of AuCoin Associates Inc., in St. Petersburg / Clearwater; James Raulerson of St. Petersburg/Clearwater Convention and Visitors Bureau (CVB); Lisa Humphrey, Public Relations (PR) Representative for the Tampa Bay CVB; Josie Gulliksen from Newman PR; Milt Adams from the Paul Smiths Adirondack Park Visitor Interpretive Center; Jonell Moodys, PR & Communications Manager of Naples, Marco Island, Everglades CVB; Everglades National Park; Big Cypress National Preserve.

Special thanks to Airtran for truly excellent airline transportation.

Thanks to Andy Flynn, Senior Public Information Specialist; and Lydia Wright, Adirondack Park Naturalist at the New York State Adirondack Park Agency Visitor Interpretive Center at Paul Smiths. And to Margaret Marchuk, Director of Media Relations, Lake Placid Essex County Visitors Bureau.

Special thanks to Judith, Weston, and Genni for watching the waters with us; David Perry, Teal Hutton, Jason Cring, and Robin Dana for their great work designing and producing this book.

INDEX

INDEX

INDEX

INDEX

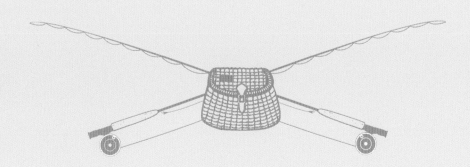

PHOTO CREDITS

Page vi courtesy of Lone Mountain Ranch; page 2-3 courtesy of Valhalla Lodge; page 4, 5 courtesy of Alaska's Boardwalk Lodge; page 10, 11 courtesy of Kirk Gay, Alaska's Valhalla Lodge; page 12 courtesy of Valhalla Lodge; page 13 courtesy of Valhalla Lodge; page 16, 21 courtesy of Dan Michels, Crystal Creek Lodge; page 22-23 courtesy of Paul Nelson Farm; page 24, 25 courtesy of Cynthia Gose, Dos Angeles Ranch; page 28, 29 courtesy of Annette Ashley, Legacy Ranch; page 32, 33 courtesy of Jessica Wipf, Paul Nelson Farm; page 36-37 courtesy of Libby Camps; page 38, 39 courtesy of Fairmont Kenauk; ; page 50, 51 courtesy of Libby Camps; page 64 courtesy of Weatherby's; page 70, 71, 75 courtesy of Dan Blanco, Flying B Ranch; page 76, 77 courtesy of Howard Mills, Minette Bay Lodge; page 82, courtesy of Morrison's Rogue River; page 86, 87 courtesy of Brandi Allen and Kenneth Boone, Three Rivers Ranch; page 90, 91 courtesy of Wapiti Meadow Ranch; page 94-95 courtesy of Big Hole Lodge; page 96, 97, 98 courtesy of Paul Wallop, Canyon Ranch; page 102, 103 courtesy of Lanette Evener, Craig Fellin Outfitters and Big Hole Lodge; page 106, 107 courtesy of Elktrout Lodge; page 110, 111 courtesy of Firehole Ranch; page 116, 117 courtesy of Lone Mountain Ranch; page 120, 121, 125 courtesy of Elizabeth Warren, Madison Valley Ranch; page 126, 127, 129, 130 courtesy of Dana Post, Paul Roos Outfitters: North Fork Crossing Lodge; page 132, 133 courtesy of Spotted Bear Ranch; page 136, 137, 141 courtesy of Keith Radabaugh, The Blue Damsel on Rock Creek; page 142, 143, 145, 147 courtesy of Three Forks Ranch; page 148, 149 courtesy of Amanda Dunn, Triple Creek Ranch; page 154-155 courtesy of Shoal Grass Lodge; page 156, 157, 161 courtesy of Blackberry Farm; page 159 courtesy of Blackberry Lodge; page 162, 163 courtesy of Marcia Greene, Chetola Resort at Blowing Rock; page 166, 167 courtesy of Tim Stull, Deer Creek Lodge; page 170, 171 courtesy of Olan Menard, Grosse Savanne Waterfowl and Wildlife Lodge; page 174, 175 courtesy of Bobby Caskey, Shoal Grass Lodge and Conference Center; page 178-179 courtesy of Pine Hill Plantation; page 180 courtesy of Carol Wightman, The Marquesa Hotel; page 188, 189 courtesy of Doug Coe, Pine Hill Plantation; page 192, 193 courtesy of Wynfield Plantation; page 198-199 courtesy of The Alisal Guest Ranch and Golf Resort; page 200, 201 courtesy of Robin Sharpe, The Alisal Guest Ranch and Golf Resort; page 206, 207 courtesy of Bruce Hanson and Sandy Macnab, Highland Hills Ranch; page 214 courtesy of Dan Monaghan, New Mexico Tourism Department; page 215 courtesy of Gus Holm, Vermejo Park Ranch; back cover photography courtesy of The Pointe in Upper Saranac Lake, New York.

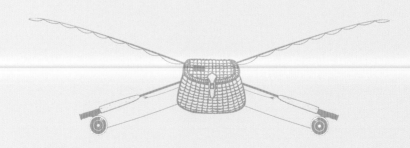